FROM EARLY VEDANTA TO KASHMIR SHAIVISM

SUNY SERIES IN RELIGIOUS STUDIES
HAROLD COWARD, EDITOR

FROM EARLY VEDANTA TO KASHMIR SHAIVISM

Gaudapada, Bhartrhari, and Abhinavagupta

Natalia Isayeva

State University of New York Press

Published by
State University of New York Press, Albany

Printed in the United States of America

For information, address State University of New York Press,
State University Plaza, Albany, N.Y., 12246

Production by Marilyn P. Semerad
Marketing by Bernadette La Manna

Library of Congress Cataloging-in-Publication Data

Isaeva, N. V.
From early Vedanta to Kashmir Shaivism : Gaudapada, Bhartrhari, and Abhinavagupta / Natalia Isayeva.
p. cm. — (SUNY series in religion.)
Includes index.
ISBN 0-7914-2449-9. — ISBN 0-7914-2450-2 (pbk.)
1. Vedanta. 2. Kashmir Śaivism—Doctrines. I. Title. II. Series.
B132.V3I73 1995
181′.48—dc20 94-38805
CIP

10 9 8 7 6 5 4 3 2 1

Contents

PART III
Further Developments: The Interplay of Energies and Artistic Creation

The Brain is wider than the Sky,
For, put them Side by Side,
The one the other will contain
With ease, and you beside.

The Brain is deeper than the Sea,
For, hold them, Blue to Blue,
The one the other will absorb,
As sponges, buckets do.

The Brain is just the weight of God,
For—heft them—Pound for Pound—
And they will differ, if they do,
As Syllable from Sound.

—Emily Dickinson

Acknowledgments

In many respects this is an unusual book. Its main subject is the philosophy of language. It deals mainly with Sanskrit texts, and it is written in English by a Russian scholar. I had to analyze inner structures of speech, its tricks and devices in a language which is not my own. The book itself was written owing to the Spalding Visiting Fellowship which enabled me to stay in Oxford for two terms—from October, 1993 until March, 1994. So, my first thanks go to the Spalding Foundation and to all the members of the Spalding Committee who elected me for this Fellowship. I am also grateful to the administration and members of Wolfson College, as well as to the Acting President, Dr. W. J. Kennedy; they made my stay there an extremely pleasant one. I might also add that when the book was almost finished, Dr. Kennedy suggested I could stay there for six more weeks in order to complete it.

I am also very grateful to my tutors at Oxford. Besides directing me in a general way, Professor Richard Gombrich was kind enough to look through the section on Gauḍapāda, adding valuable comments. My thanks go to his wife, Dr. Sanjukta Gupta, for her warmth and understanding, as well as for her inspiring talks on Indian drama. I was greatly impressed by the brilliant lectures of Professor Alexis Sanderson: they helped me to clarify many obscure points in Kashmir Śaivism. I am also thankful to Dr. Jim Benson, who was lecturing on grammar theory of Ancient India and agreed to read the section on Bhartṛhari, checking some of the quotations and suggesting ways to improve the text.

I am infinitely grateful to the Director of SUNY Press, Mr. William Eastman. He and his colleagues believed in me when I myself was far from being confident. Many thanks to

Dr. Harold Coward for his deep and perceptive remarks on the manuscript. Many thanks to the production editor, Marilyn Semerad, and to the copy editor who, I am sure, had a lot of trouble going through this difficult and often obscure text.

I remember all my colleagues and friends in Oxford: their generosity and their kind-heartedness helped me more than I can ever tell.

I am thankful to my flatmate at Wolfson, Dr. Jennifer Moreton, who became my friend and with whom I could discuss certain aspects of Christian theology. I remember with pleasure the talks on dramatic art we had with Professor Michael Gearin-Tosh from St. Catherine's College. I am also grateful to my London friend, a specialist on William Blake, Mr. Tim Heath, who, with truly British patience and reserve, listened to my endless monologues in broken and faulty English. And my thanks go to my husband, Sergei, who listened to the Russian version of some of the passages. Incidentally, certain ideas of the book indirectly stem from our joint work on Russian translations of Søren Kierkegaard's works (primarily, "Either/Or" and "Concluding Unscientific Postscript").

To all of them I owe a debt of gratitude. And, needless to say, the faults of the book (which, in spite of all their effort, remain numerous) are entirely mine.

Introduction

The book deals with early Vedānta, that is, a pre-Śaṅkara Vedānta, which was characterized by a deeply ingrained belief in the power of the word, when the higher reality was often approached through painstaking grammatical studies. It presented an exquisite analysis of consciousness and, at the same time, often relied on esoteric meditation practice verging on Tāntrism. It was powerfully influenced by Buddhism, and yet, had an equally powerful sense of being rooted in Brahmanical orthodoxy. Judging from these different views, early Vedānta was nothing but a tangled mess of poorly disguised contradictions. Of course, in just a few centuries, the gap dividing these early Vedāntic teachings from Śaṅkara's mature Vedānta was bridged; roughly moulded joints and connections were smoothed down, harsh contrasts were resolved within the all-embracing fold of Advaita Vedānta.

Yet one cannot totally escape the feeling that in every synthesis, in every harmony, however perfect it might be, something is missing. Every time philosophers try to bring together or connect diverse trends of thought, something is sacrificed, often the more colourful and intricate details, more exquisite embellishments. And it is often the case that those very details, presumed to be purely ornamental and superfluous, could have given birth to new ideas and theoretical notions.

Śaṅkara's Advaita Vedānta is undoubtedly an impressive enough philosophy, an elaborate pyramid of escalating concepts and images. Let us take a look at some of the foundational elements that ultimately came to be discarded—perhaps they were necessary and indispensable only for the initial stages of its consruction. We naturally want to take a closer look at Śaṅkara's predecessors, at his forerunners who were trying to propound their own ideas about God, the creation of the universe, or the nature of the human soul.

This book deals mainly with the ideas and teaching of Gauḍapāda, the teacher of Śaṅkara's master, Govinda, and with the ideas of the grammarian and philosopher, Bhartṛhari. In my view, these two thinkers should be regarded as predecessors of certain schools of non-dualistic Kashmir Śaivism, which proved to be quite theistical in their essence, rather than immediate forerunners of Śaṅkara's Vedānta.

Generally speaking, the concepts of early Vedāntins became natural bridges or links which connected the Advaita system to other religious and philosophical systems. It is well known, for instance, that Maṇḍanamiśra was deeply attracted to Mīmāṃsā point of view. At first glance, Gauḍapāda presents a phenomenal example of a mediation between orthodox Vedānta and "heretical" notions of Buddhism. Meanwhile, Bhartṛhari, probably the most interesting and original philosopher of the whole pre-Śaṅkara orthodox tradition, succeeded in using some of the Buddhist ideas, as well as in supplying a necessary link between the emerging Advaita Vedānta and a venerable grammar tradition of ancient India. Finally, all of these early Vedāntins were much more proficient than their relatively moderate successor in blending philosophical concepts with the religious, mystical, and ritualistic side of their respective teachings. Again, Bhartṛhari seems to provide the most compelling example of that blending, since his theoretical tastes and prophetic revelations have found themselves a direct continuation within the fold of various mystical and Tāntric schools of non-dualist Kashmir Śaivism.

But however colourful and interesting these ritualistic traits might have been in their own right, it was nevertheless absolutely necessary to anchor the recurrent mythological and psychological images of early Vedānta in a solid ontological foundation; it was important to show their compelling and indispensable character, as well as to determine a possible direction of their eventual development. In fact, when analyzing the notions and concepts of any religious and philosophical school, one should always try to look for ontological implications, even if the latter did not seem to be entirely transparent to the adepts themselves. And that inevitably calls for certain interpretations, certain additional suggestions that might contribute towards revealing the inner logical structure of the system in question.

When looking at Gauḍapāda's system, it is immediately clear that instead of the two levels of reality and consciousness singled out by Śaṅkara (that is, *vyāvahārika-vidyā*, or "the knowledge of empirical practice," and *pāramārthika-vidyā*, or "the higher knowledge"), instead of dealing with an opposition between the pure *ātman* and the world, we are confronted with a fourfold structure of the universe. And although it was Gauḍapāda who introduced the notion of *māyā*, or "cosmic illusion," into the teaching of Vedānta, one cannot escape the impression that his vision of the world was based not so much upon the concept of pure reality, devoid of any attributes and characteristics, as on something fuller, more multi-dimensional, and dynamic. In a lot of present-day Indological studies, Gauḍapāda is presented as a thinker who was mainly engaged in establishing possible correlations between, respectively, the "microcosm" of a human soul in its manifold apperances, and the "macrocosm" of universal ontological and even cosmological structures. And, according to many Indologists, it was precisely this notion that prevented him from reaching the higher stages of Advaita thought, for it contaminated his pure ontological outlook with traces of psychological and overt mythological traits. That is why some argue that even though Gauḍapāda became the first Vedāntin to suggest an opposition between the higher reality of Brahman and a relative, limited reality of an illusory dream, he still could not successfully integrate the concept of pure consciousness, which later came to form the core of Śaṅkara's "mature"Advaita.

In this work I approach Gauḍapāda's teachings with a slightly different attitude. In my opinion, a shift in the angle of consideration, a new line of inquiry might reveal more coherent explanations for concepts and notions that would otherwise bewilder an unbiased reader. I am suggesting that the key to some of Gauḍapāda's more extravagant affirmations concerning the nature of reality is most likely to be found in his approach to the universal dynamic process—the process which ultimately leads both to the emergence of the world and to the fourfold structuring of consciousness.

It is well known that in Śaṅkara's Advaita the higher Brahman is pure and devoid of form (*arūpa*), while all of its temporary "attributes," "qualities," and "forms" are merely passing and accidental (*āgantuka*). They are nothing more than superficial characteristics superimposed on pure consciousness, due either to our limited means of logical reasoning, or to our disturbed and obscured sensibility. Meanwhile, for another early Vedāntin, Bhartṛhari, Brahman is posited as Speech (*vāk*), the Word (*śabda*); Brahman has a definite outline, he looms as a peculiar emerging shape. Once can also say that within the boundaries of our universe this entity is represented by the Vedas. A Vedic text can and should be essentially regarded as Brahman himself—as Brahman who is turning around to face or address us. Certainly, for both Gauḍapāda and Bhartṛhari, Brahman must always remain one and the same. According to the orthodox Indian tradition, Brahman is a totally uniform, homogenous and unchanging entity, in which no differentiation can ever be discerned. However, from the point of view of the early Vedāntins, the "seeds" (*bīja*) of the forthcoming division of this entity are already present within this unity. But they are so deeply "folded in," so securely hidden in their latent existence, that one can only sense their presence owing to the inherent tension that eventually brings them forth. In this respect, Bhartṛhari no longer depicts Brahman as the pure, quiet light of consciousness, but rather as a tightly compressed spring, which, by its nature and inherent tension, will unfold or straighten up.

Brahman is one and the same, but, according to the early Vedāntins, when this compressed spring is finally released, the world—which is created or manifested by Brahman—becomes manifold and diverse. Brahman is one and the same, but we, essentially finite and limited creatures, contained within that perceptible universe, we are able to conceive of it only through approximations, interpretations, and mental constructions (*vikalpa*). The most condensed form of Brahman for both Gauḍapāda and Bhartṛhari is the sacred syllable *Oṃ* (*praṇava*). Vedic texts undoubtedly provide us with a true image, a true reflection of Brahman, but the core and the initial "seed" (*bīja*) of the Veda, its true form, as well as its least deceptive embodiment, is represented in this world by the continuous pulsation (*spanda*) of the sacred mantra.

The teachings of Bhartṛhari are also considered from a different viewpoint and largely re-interpreted through the course of this book. The aim of this approach was to link Bhartṛhari with the tradition of non-dualist Kashmir Śaivism in a more natural and convincing way. It certainly became increasingly clear—at least to me, while I was writing this book—how within the notion of Brahman as pure consciousness one begins to discern, more and more vividly, the shaping up of a new image; how through all the entanglements of complex philosophical definitions one can see the emerging face of a personified God. The systems of Bhartṛhari and Gauḍapāda provided the Vedānta philosophical system with a new element that could eventually lead an adept (*sādhaka*) to the concept of God endowed with a name, and not just a nameless and pure Brahman. These schools succeeded in providing an ontological ground for the notion of a dynamic, active, and potent God—the God who creates this world in a loosing forth of energy, through his own artistic and poetic effort.

While I agree with some authors, who (like André Padoux) argue that the process of "Brahmanization" or "Vedantization" of Kashmir Śaivism, can be traced from the beginning of the ninth century A.D.,[1] it is also quite appropriate to assume that even earlier than that (beginning in the fifth-sixth century) one could witness a complementary process going on in the opposite direction, when religious paradigms were directly influencing philosophical constructions. To my

1. See: André Padoux. *Vāc: The Concept of the Word in Selected Hindu Tantras* (Albany: SUNY Press, 1990), 32-33.

mind, both Gauḍapāda and Bhartṛhari clearly demonstrate the possibilities of Tāntric developments within the scope of Vedānta religious philosophy. I believe that my approach to early Vedānta enabled me to find more plausible solutions for some of the technical and specific problems inherent in these teachings: for example, it provided useful keys for explaining Bhartṛhari's attitude towards Vedic injunctions (*vidhi*), as well as for determining their role in his system.

Finally, I think that the teaching of Bhartṛhari definitely differs and perhaps deliberately steers away from the Neoplatonic ontology and cosmology peculiar to the religious and philosophical systems of Kashmir Śaivism. For Abhinavagupta, as well as for other non-dualist Kashmir Śaivites, the initial light of creation inevitably splits up and divides when it begins its downward journey; and, at the same time, it becomes more dense, assuming increasingly less and less transparent manifestations within the hierarchy of the created universe. In contrast, Bhartṛhari is still more inclined to oscillate between the notions of "pure," qualityless Brahman (*nirguṇa brahma*) and Brahman endowed with qualities and powers (*saguṇa brahma*). Bhartṛhari avoids constructing endless cosmological and psychological hierarchies (a process that, theoretically speaking, can be carried on ad infinitum); he prefers to reason on the level of energies. Curiously enough, the most striking similarities were probably those that linked the ontological notions of Bhartṛhari with the corresponding tenets of the Kashmir Śaivite theory of aesthetics. In this respect, one is first and foremost reminded of the concept of "suggested meaning" (*dhvani*) and that of the aesthetical pleasure, or "tasting" (*rasa*), propounded by Abhinavagupta.

And this similarity, on the whole, brings us within reach of a somewhat different theistic tradition. Strange as it might sound, the closest counterparts for the early Vedānta ideas can be found in the teaching of medieval Byzantine Hesychasts, Gregory of Nyssa and Gregory Palamas, and, possibly, in the concepts of the Russian Orthodox *imyaslaviye* system of Pavel Florensky and Alexei Losev. The comparison might seem a bit far-fetched, even though there are distinct parallels between

Kashmir Śaivism and Neoplatonic teachings. In fact, when I suggested in this book that some notions of Christian theology might remind us of ideas present in early Vedānta, I merely ventured to touch on the extreme points where the two systems seemed to resemble each other. I never held that there was a point where they actually coincided; in my opinion, there is no way to obliterate the differences or bridge the tremendous gap between Christianity and Indian thought. However, sometimes it is worthwhile to follow the parallel paths taken by certain ideas as they developed in different systems. And one might well recall that such a keen and discerning scholar as Paul Hacker went to great lengths trying to establish correspondences between Śaṅkara's Advaita and Neoplatonism,[2] even though the grounds for this analogy were certainly less convincing than a possibility of a common reference point between non-dualist Śaivite teachings and some corresponding Neoplatonic insights and ideas. In any case, the concept of "energy," derived from a medieval Christian tradition, proved useful for a new outlook on early Vedānta, as well as for a novel interpretation of Abhinavagupta's aesthetic theory.

---

2. See, for example, his essay on the concept of consciousness in Śaṅkara's teaching and Neoplatonism, where he says, by way of conclusion, that "in spite of the enormous disparity of the two cultures we found in the two systems an impressive number of terms that are partly almost literally translatable, partly interpretable as different ways of pointing to the same intended reality." —Paul Hacker, "'Cit' and 'Nous,'" in his *Kleine Schriften*, herausgegeben und erläutert von Lambert Schmithausen (Wiesbaden: Franz Steiner Verlag, 1977), S.336.

Note on Sources

Sanskrit passages from the texts of Gauḍapāda and Bhartṛhari are cited from the following editions:

1. *Iśādidaśopaniṣadaḥ: Śāṅkarabhāṣyasametaḥ. Ten Principal Upanishads with Śāṅkarabhāṣya* (Delhi, Varanasi, and Patna: Motilal Banarsidass, 1964).
2. Bhartṛhari. *Vākya-padīya, Brahma-kaṇḍa*, edited by Prof. K. V. Abhyankar and Acarya V. P. Limaye (Poona: Sadhana Press, 1965).

I have also used existing English translations of Gauḍapāda's *Kārikās*:

1. *The Māṇḍūkyopaniṣad with Gauḍapāda's Kārikās and the Bhāṣya of Śaṅkara*, translated into English by Manilal N. Dvivedi (Bombay: Bombay Theosophical Publication Fund, 1909).
2. *The Māṇḍūkyopanishad with Gauḍapāda's Kārikā and Śaṅkara's Commentary*, translated and annotated by Swami Nikhilananda, with a foreword by V. Subrahmanya Iyer (Mysore: Sri Ramakrishna Ashrama, 1949).
3. Gauḍapāda, *Māṇḍūkya-kārikā: Eight Upanishads, with the Commentary of Śaṅkarācārya*, edited and translated by Swami Gambhirananda, volume two (Calcutta: Advaita Ashrama, 1978).

I also made considerable use of two translations of Bhartṛhari's text:

1. K. A. Subramania Iyer, *The Vākyapadīya of Bhartṛhari with the Vṛtti*. (Poona: Deccan College, 1965).
2. Madeleine Biardeau, *Bhartṛhari. Vākyapadīya Brahmakaṇḍa avec la Vṛtti de Harivṛṣabha*, Traduction, introduction et notes par Madeleine Biardeau (Paris: Editions E. de Boccard, 1964).

However, mostly (when not otherwise cited) I supply my own translations of the texts concerned.

I Gauḍapāda

The Mind and the Cosmos: Reflection or Prototype?

1 Gauḍapāda: Life and Works

The "great teacher" Gauḍapāda is one of the most venerated sages of the early Vedānta tradition; it is generally assumed that he is separated from Śaṅkara by at least one generation of preceptors. In the final passage of his commentary on Gauḍapāda's magnum opus, the *Māṇḍūkya-kārikā*, Śaṅkara pays tribute to him as his *parama-guru*, that is, either as a "great teacher," or as the "teacher of [his] teacher." In fact, passages from the *Māṇḍūkya-kārikā* are cited almost verbatim in Śaṅkara's *Commentary on the Brahma-sūtra* (*Māṇḍūkya-kārikā*, 1.16, is referred to in *Brahma-sūtra-bhāṣya*, 2.1.9, while the reference to the *kārikā* 3.15 is found in *Brahma-sūtra-bhāṣya*, 1.4.14). Though Gauḍapāda is not named in Śaṅkara's *Commentary on the Brahma-sūtra*, he is nonetheless hailed as a great "knower of the Vedānta tradition" (*vedānta-saṃpradāya-vid*). We can also find a reference to Gauḍapāda in Śaṅkara's *Commentary on the Śvetāśvatara Upanishad*, where it is stated that Gauḍapāda was a pupil of another renowned Vedānta sage, Śuka.[1] There is also the testimony of one of Śaṅkara's closest disciples, Sureśvara, who cites Gauḍapāda's *Māṇḍūkya-kārikā* in his work *Naiṣkārmya-siddhi* ("The Realization of [the state of] Non-action"),[2] as well as in his commentary on Śaṅkara's *Bṛhadāraṇyakopaniṣad-*

1. See Śaṅkara, *Śvetāśvataropaniṣad-bhāṣya*, 1.8: tathā ca śukaśiṣyo gauḍapādācāryaḥ / ("and thus [it was said] by the teacher Gauḍapāda, the disciple of Śuka").

2. See *Naiṣkārmya-siddhi*, 4.41, where Sureśvara cites from the *Māṇḍūkya-kārikā* (hereinafter referred to as MK), 1.11, and *Naiṣkārmya-siddhi*, 4.42, where he introduces a passage from MK, 1.15. In

bhāṣya.[3] Both passages from Gauḍapāda's *Kārikās* and occasionally his name, keep cropping up in later Vedānta works,[4] the context usually being that of deepest veneration.

The very name of the Vedānta preceptor is known to us in several versions; apart from the most popular form of 'Gauḍapāda', favoured by Śaṅkara, there are close variations such as 'Gauḍācarana',[5] 'Gauḍapādācārya' (Śaṅkara's *Commentary on Śvetāśvatara Upanishad*, 1.8), 'Gauḍācārya' (Vidyāraṇya's *Pañca-daśī* ["The Five Chapters"], 2.23), and simply 'Gauḍa' (Sureśvara, *Naiṣkārmya-siddhi*, 4.44).

It is difficult to say anything definite about Gauḍapāda's life, since—as is the case with most early Indian religious teachers—the only available information is derived either from hagiographies or from scanty references in other works. In the living tradition of oral instruction in Vedic knowledge, Gauḍapāda is considered to be the teacher of Śaṅkara's own master, Govinda. A later Advaitin, Ānandagiri, who wrote his own commentary (*Ṭīkā*) on Śaṅkara's commentary to *Māṇḍūkya-kārikā*, notes at the beginning of his text that Gauḍapāda started his spiritual quest with a long penance (*tapas*) deep in the Himalayas, at Badarikāśrama, which was considered to be the sacred residence of the Lord Nara-Nārāyaṇa. Having pleased

---

Jñanottama's gloss to the text of Sureśvara, the passage is identified as "the saying of Gauḍapāda" (*gauḍapādīya-vākya*). See Colin A. Cole, *Asparśa-yoga: A Study of Gauḍapāda's Māṇḍūkya Kārikā* (Delhi: Motilal Banarsidass, 1982), 3-4.

3. See Sureśvara, *Bṛhadāraṇyakopaniṣad-bhāṣya-vārttika*, 1.4.389 (with the reference to *gauḍapādīya-vācas*—"the words of Gauḍapāda") as well as 2.1.386 and 4.4.886.

4. To name only a few instances: Vidyāraṇya, *Pañca-daśī*, 2.28 and 2.29; Sadānanda, *Vedānta-sāra*; Maṇḍanamiśra, *Brahma-siddhi*, etc. See more details in Cole, *Asparśa-yoga*, 4.

5. This version is found in Bālakṛṣṇānanda's *Śārīraka-mīmāṃsā-bhāṣya-vārttika*, 2.9-12. See T. M. P. Mahadevan, *Gauḍapāda: A Study in Early Advaita* (Madras: University of Madras Press, 1957), 7-8; Cole, *Asparśa-yoga*, 4.

the Lord with his perseverence, Gauḍapāda obtained permission to propound the tenets of Advaita Vedānta. Many believe that he received his preliminary instruction in this system from the legendary sage Śuka. After that period of study, Gauḍapāda composed his commentary on the *Māṇḍūkya Upanishad.* According to the testimony of a later Advaitin, Bālakṛṣṇānanda (seventeenth century), Gauḍapāda was originally one of the esteemed masters of the Gauḍas, who lived on the banks of the river Hirarāvatī (probably, North Bengal).[6] So it is quite possible that Gauḍapāda was named after his people, or ethnic group, with the *pāda*, a common honorific, added later.

For many years, scholars believed that Gauḍapāda lived about the seventh century (based upon the assumed date for Śaṅkara, 780-820, since he precedes Śaṅkara by approximately a century). However, after Śaṅkara's date was shifted to an earlier time, it was felt that the same should apply to Gauḍapāda. V. Bhattacharya and T. M. P. Mahadevan[7] both suggested that a much more plausible date for Gauḍapāda's life should be about A.D. 500.[8] Their assumption was largely based upon the testimony of some Buddhist texts. For instance, Bhāvaviveka in his *Tarka-jvala* ("The Jewel of Reasoning"), the autocommentary on his *Mādhyamika-hṛdaya-kārikā* ("The Kārikās on the Heart of Mādhyamika [Teaching]"), 8.10-13, cites passages extremely close to the *Māṇḍūkya-kārikā*. And literal passages from the *Māṇḍūkya-kārikā* are found in Śāntarakṣita's *Tattva-saṅgraha* ("The Collection [of Writings] on the Essence [of Learning]"), 93, while his pupil, Kamalaśīla, in his commentary *Pañjikā*, identifies them as *upaniṣat*

---

6. Bālakṛṣṇānanda, *Śārīraka-mīmāṃsā-bhāṣya-vārttika*, 2.9-12. See T. M. P. Mahadevan, *Gauḍapāda*, 8-9; R. D. Karmakar, ed. *Gauḍapāda-kārikā*, translation and notes (Poona: Bhandarkar Oriental Institute Press, 1953), iv.

7. See Mahadevan, *Gauḍapāda*, 309.

8. See V. Bhattacharya, ed. and tr., The Āgamaśāstra of Gauḍapāda (Poona: 1943, lxxv-lxxviii; Mahadevan, *Gauḍapāda*, 13-15.

śāstra—"the teaching of the Upanishads." Since Śāntarakṣita's date is definitely ascertained from the Tibetan sources (705-762), this sets the latest limit for Gauḍapāda's date. And since Gauḍapāda himself is citing passages that sound very much like Nāgārjuna and Asaṅga, the earliest date could not be set before A.D. 400. In other words, most scholars now seem to agree that the probable date of Gauḍapāda's writing is the fifth or the very beginning of the sixth century.[9]

Gauḍapāda's most prominent work is, undoubtedly, his commentary on the *Māṇḍūkya Upanishad*, or *Māṇḍūkya-kārikā*. The metrical treatise *Māṇḍūkya-kārikā* is also known under the names 'Gauḍapāda-kārikā', 'Gauḍapādīya-kārikā' ("The Kārikās of Gauḍapāda"), and 'Āgama-śāstra' ("The Śāstra on the Sacred Text"). Gauḍapāda has also written a commentary (*Bhāṣya*) on Īśvarakṛṣṇa's *Sāṅkhya-kārikā*, as well as another commentary (*Vṛtti*) on *Uttara-gītā*. Sometimes Gauḍapāda is cited as the author of a number of Tāntric works, including *Subhāgodaya-stuti* and *Śrī-vidyāraṇya-sūtra*. In Vedāntic tradition, he is also believed to have written other independent works and commentaries, but there is no evidence to substantiate this.[10]

---

9. See *Asparśa-yoga*, 7-8.

10. See R. D. Karmarkar, *Gauḍapāda-Kārikā*, v-x, as well as the general enumeration of his works in Cole, *Asparśa-yoga*, 7-10.

2 *Māṇḍūkya-kārikā:* The Gradations of Consciousness

In this part of the book we will focus on Gauḍapāda's *Māṇḍūkya-kārikā*. It is a remarkable work which encompasses the philosophical notions of early Vedānta and their religious imlications. In his book on Gauḍapāda's *asparśa-yoga* (lit., "yoga free of touches, of contacts"), Colin A. Cole wanted "to point out the essential soteriological concern and purpose of Gauḍapāda's teachings as expounded in the 'Māṇḍūkya Kārikā'." He writes: "The term 'teachings' is used here to indicate the underlying religio-spiritual dimensions of this text. For the text embodies several elements of the Indian soteriological quest. Philosophy, metaphysics, epistemology, psychology and religion are all blended under this essential concern."[11] While fully sympathizing with these words and Cole's attempt to bring together metaphysical tenets and their religious contents, I have a somewhat different idea of Gauḍapāda's ontological premises as presented in his *Māṇḍūkya-kārikā*.

The treatise itself is divided into four "chapters" (*prakaraṇa*). The first one, "Āgama-prakaraṇa," the subtitle of which is sometimes extended to the entire text, is in fact an extensive commentary on the *Māṇḍūkya Upanishad* (*Māṇḍūkyopaniṣad*). Strangely, the text of the latter, in the form of twelve prose passages, is completely included in the *Māndūkya-kārikā* and does not exist separately from

---

11. Cole, *Asparśa-yoga*, 134.

Gauḍapāda's work. Some Western Indologists, in particular Paul Deussen, even have gone so far as to suggest that this Upanishad, believed to have been written later than most of the others, was actually composed by Gauḍapāda. This somewhat extravagant hypothesis does not fit the main tenets of Vedāntic orthodoxy, which consistently and absolutely distinguishes between "sacred revelation" (that is, Vedic texts, considered to be *śruti*, or divinely "heard") and "sacred tradition" (that is, interpretations proposed by human philosophers and thinkers and regarded as *smṛti*, or something "remembered"). Yet the Vaishnavite tradition of Vedānta (mainly the followers of Rāmānuja and Madhva), on the contrary, substantially reduces the contribution of Gauḍapāda, suggesting that the whole of the first chapter of *Māṇḍūkya-kārikā*, including the verse interpretation of the prose passages, constitutes the *Māṇḍūkya Upanishad.*

So, the first chapter of Gauḍapāda's work is called "Āgama-prakaraṇa," that is, "a chapter on the sacred text." It starts with a detailed analysis of consciousness. Gauḍapāda tries to follow the four states (*avasthā*) of consciousness; according to another interpretation, they are the four "steps" (*pāda*) that are to be taken in order to achieve liberation. These four steps or four elements of a united whole might be also represented as four "feet" of an animal, namely, as four feet of a sacred cow (or a she-buffalo), which personifies sacred Speech (*vāk*), essentially posited at the very origins of creation.[12] And one might recall that in Indian prosody *pāda*

12. See: T. Ya. Elizarenkova, *Yazyk i stil vediyskikh rishi* (Language and Style of the Vedic Rishis) (Moscow: Nauka [Vostochnaya literatura], 1993), 111-12. Incidentally, when considering the four feet of the sacred cow, or pimordial Speech (*vāk*), we might also remember that her udder has four teats that provide living beings with the four-streamed flow of Vedas. Nevertheless, in his *Commentary on Māṇḍūkya Upanishad*, 2, Śaṅkara specifies that "the four quarters [should be understood] like the four quarters of a Kārṣāpana coin, and not like the four feet of the cow" (catuṣpatkārṣāpanavan na gaur iva). Śaṅkara, however, professed little interest in the Goddess of Speech.

is also the term to signify a line of verse.

The first state, which is familiar to everybody, is defined as *viśva*, or as "belonging to everyone," a "universal" state. It is the ordinary state of wakefulness (*jāgarita*), of mundane perception, where our consciousness perceives (in Sanskrit philosophical terminology, "enjoys"—*bhuñjate*) external objects. In the words of Gauḍapāda himself,

> The universal [one]
> enjoys external objects,
> and is all-pervasive . . .[13]
> (*Māṇḍūkya-kārikā*, 1.1)

Here we encounter the normal, everyday activity of the senses (*indriya*) and the "organs of action" (*karmendriya*);[14] the behaviour of human beings at this level is centered on external objects and is governed by the norms of the community and pragmatic logic.

The second "step" taken by consciousness is when it enters the state of dreaming (*svapna*). In the text of *Māṇḍūkya*

---

13. MK, 1.1: Bahiṣprajño vibhur viśvo . . .

14. As specified in *Māṇḍūkya Upanishad*, 3, consciousness in the ordinary, waking state makes use of "seven limbs" (*sapta-aṅga*). If one is to abide by the usual enumeration valid for the Agnihotra rite, these seven limbs are: the head, the eyes, the living breaths, the stomach, the bladder, the legs, and the mouth (*Chāndogya Upanishad*, 5.18.2: "Since heaven is truly Vaiśvanāra's head, the sun is his eyes, air is his pranas; space, his stomach; water, his bladder; earth, his legs . . . the fire Āhavanīya is verily his mouth"). From this we can see that the organs or the parts of the human body come to be associated with respective "elements" of the material universe. Besides those "limbs," consciousness has "nineteen mouths" (*ekonaviṃśati-mukha*): five organs of sense (*buddhi-indriya*), five organs of action (*karma-indryia*), five *prāṇas* or "living breaths," a mind (*manas*), an intellectual will (*buddhi*), a personal ego (*ahaṅkara*), as well as the process of consciousness itself (*citta*); they are called the "mouths," because they are regarded as the "doors of perception" that help to grasp, or "enjoy," the sense objects.

Upanishad and, correspondingly, in the first chapter of *Māṇḍūkya-kārikā*, this dream state is called "the shining one" (*taijasa*). According to Gauḍapāda,

> . . . the shining one
> enjoys internal [objects].[15]
> (*Māṇḍūkya-kārikā*, 1.1)

The "internal" objects presented here are produced by consciousness itself in the form of mental images, memories, dreams. This sage also embraces all "illusory," fantastic, and delusive perceptions that cannot be verified or checked by ordinary experience. We could assume that consciousness here is shining forth with a sort of reflected light, fueled by its former sensations and the skills acquired in the course of life. However, Gauḍapāda shifts the semantic emphasis: for him, consciousness is posited as a "shining" one since all its external, gross envelopes are already torn away and the thin sheath of the dream state is incapable of blocking out the inner light, which shines forth from the depths of *ātman*.

However, just like consciousness in its waking state, a "shining" consciousness makes active use of all its tools and instruments. Following the line of reasoning suggested by the author of the Upanishad, Gauḍapāda explains that even at this stage (as with the first) we can enumerate "seven limbs" (*sapta-aṅga*), that is, bodily organs or bodily functions, as well as "nineteen mouths" (*eko-naviṃśati-mukha*).[16] The nineteen "mouths," or "doors of perception," comprise the usual set of five "organs of sense" (*buddhi-indriya*), five "organs of action"

---

15. MK, 1.1: Hy antaḥprājñas tu taijasaḥ /

16. According to *Māṇḍūkya Upanishad*, 4, consciousness, in its dreaming state, makes use of the same tools and instruments that are employed in a waking state: it also has its "seven limbs" and "nineteen mouths." This is a clear indication that all these "instruments" of consciousness are not a set of physical characteristics, but rather "abilities," "potentialities," and "powers" of consciousness that can come into play at any moment.

(*karma-indriya*), five "living forces" (*prāṇa*), a three-fold "inner organ" (*antaḥ-karaṇa*), which in its turn is composed of *buddhi* or "intellect," *manas* or the integrator of perceptive data, and *ahaṅkara*, that is, a feeling of one's inner ego, individual personality, the last, nineteenth element being the process of consciousness itself (*citta*). All of these functions, qualities, or attributes of consciousness (which we can regard as mental "tools"), are in themselves absolutely unconscious. They might be regarded as external and "bodily" envelopes of *ātman*—just as we are prone to regard the bodies it assumes in numerous incarnations. They are, so to speak, the "doors of perception," or, rather, the tentacles or tendrils that the *ātman* likes to shoot forth and move around in order to feel and grasp the objects that surround it. Drawing a modern analogy, we might assume them to be akin to computer hardware and software: a computer can, on no account, be regarded as "alive" or "conscious," and, similarly, all these tools and instruments are simply being used by the pure consciousness, the *ātman*. Actually, from the point of view of Advaita Vedānta, this analogy is deficient in only one respect: the technical equipment which is used by the *ātman* is totally illusory; it is invented, "dreamed of" by the conscious effort of its user. If we approach it from the angle of "absolute truth" (*pāramārthika-satyam*), we can easily see that there are neither objects of analysis or perception, nor a software program for their restructuring, nor, for that matter, any instruments of perception.

Until the illusory nature of these entities becomes evident, the instruments of perception go on dealing with the objects of the external world (which happens when the *ātman* is realized as "universal," *viśva*), as well as with the "invented" objects produced by this consciousness (which takes place at the stage of the "shining" consciousness, that is, in a dream). The border between these two groups of objects marks the difference between the first and the second "step," between the first and the second "quarter."

The third state of consciousness, or its third "step," leads us to the realm of a dreamless, deep sleep (*supti, suṣupti*). It is a sleep which is usually termed "slow sleep" in the jargon of present-day psychology. (Correspondingly, the previous stage might be labelled "quick sleep," which is characterized by the ability of consciousness to generate images.) The corresponding stage, where the *ātman* is being placed now, is called a "conscious" (*prājña*) stage; in the words of the *Māṇḍūkya Upanishad*, everything here "becomes indistinct," being a mere "lump of consciousness" (*prājña-ghana*).[17] The same idea is reiterated in *Māṇḍūkya-kārikā* which offers its commentary on the passage (1.1-5).

While, at the previous stages, consciousness was still making use of its specific instruments or tools, at the third stage the tools are involved, they continue their existence merely in a latent form. One could see them as peculiar and dangerous weapons which are safely sheathed away. Now, instead of dealing with a lot of "external" or "internal" objects, consciousness relates to the one and only feeling—an ineffable bliss (*ānanda*). The tentacles are drawn in, the doors of perception are tightly shut, consciousness has turned within and is now left to enjoy its own nature. This state is still far from the ideal state of oneness; it is still only a premonition, a foretaste of the real bliss to come. At the third stage, the *ātman* is only for a moment allowed to sweep aside the curtain of *māyā*, to peep under its veil. But this moment is enough to produce the feeling of infinite joy and serenity, and the sense of infinite possibilities.

In order to warn, and possibly brace, the adept against any temptation to remain at the stage of this "conscious" *ātman* (dreamless sleep), Gauḍapāda notes that the third "step" not only falls short of infinite bliss—it is also identical with "deep slumber" (*nidrā*). The idea here is not that this stage of consciousness is beset with illusions, but that the one and only true light cannot really shine forth from the depths of deep sleep. It is not a full liberation; at most it is a liberation from illusions, a peculiar "negative," apophatic enlightenment. A Buddhist thinker might be quite content with such a description of *nirvāṇa*, since *nirvāṇa*, or "extinguishing," is essentially regarded as a calming

---

17. MK, 1.1: Ghanaprājñas tathāprājña . . . /

down, a quieting of vain and painful activity. However, an orthodox Vedāntin cannot set out for this goal, for it comes dangerously close to complete negation and annulment. A Vedāntin would always opt for ontological guarantees of salvation, for guarantees of the real existence of the *ātman*, which is considered to be something more than an embellished metaphor for nothingness. Whatever objects are present, whatever feelings are aroused, consciousness remains the foundation of every experience and perception, the basic principle of life itself.[18]

With the fourth "step," we ultimately reach the top of the pyramid. One should bear in mind, though, that since we are still dealing with strictly phenomenal states of consciousness, that is, with something that might be experienced and realized within the sphere of this phenomenal universe, the fourth "step" means yet another and closer approach towards the nature of the *ātman*. It is not yet identical with ultimate liberation: that becomes feasible only after every possibility of coming back is destroyed. This fourth stage is a state of consciousness devoid of ills and fears. Most importantly, it has a clearly defined ontological status: as a kind of a potency or implicit possibility inherently present in all living beings. As Gauḍapāda writes:

> God the ruler is inexhaustible
> in [the task] of destruction
> of all sorrows,
> The non-dual bliss,
> this "fourth" [state],
> is said to pervade
> all beings [without exception].[19]
> (*Māṇḍūkya-kārikā*, 1.10)

---

18. As Śaṅkara says in his commentary on MK, 5, "just as [the heat of the] fire does not grow or subside with the burning of its object, the wood and so on, [but remains essentially the same,] so nothing is added or taken away [from the *ātman*] by the [experience] of its objects"—"na hi yasya yo viṣayaḥ sa tena hīyate vardhate vā na hy agniḥ svaviṣayaṃ dagdhvā kaṣṭhādi tadvat /"

19. MK, 1.10:

Turīya, literally, the "fourth" state of consciousness, is a state where there is no distinction, no opposition between something "external" and "internal," between waking and dreaming, between lightness and darkness, between joy and anguish. It is not by mere chance that in *Māṇḍūkya-kārikā* this state lacks a proper term to designate its nature, that it is referred to merely by an ordinal numeral. The "fourth" state cannot be determined or signified; it is evoked only apophatically, through a series of mutually contradicting definitions, that is, only in terms of a negative theology. Even in the text of the *Māṇḍūkya Upanishad* it is described with a long list of negations:

> They consider the "fourth" to be that which does not perceive the internal, does not perceive the external, does not perceive them both; and it is not a lump of consciousness—it is neither a consciousness nor its absence. It is unseen, it lies beyond the sphere of ordinary practice, it cannot be grasped, cannot be defined, cannot be thought, cannot be described.[20]
>
> (*Māṇḍūkya Upanishad*, 7)

In Gauḍapāda's interpretation the corresponding *kārikā* runs as follows:

> These two, the "universal"
> and the "shining" ones,
> are considered to be bound
> by the cause and the effect.
> The "conscious" one
> is bound only by the cause,

Nivṛtteḥ sarvaduḥkhānām īśānaḥ prabhur avyayaḥ /
Advaitaḥ sarvabhāvānāṃ devas turyo vibhuḥ smṛtaḥ //

20. "nāntaḥprajñaṃ na bahiḥprajñaṃ nobhayataprajñaṃ na prajñānaghanaṃ na prajñaṃ nāprajñam / adṛṣṭam avyavahāryam agrahyam alakṣaṇam acintyam avayapadeśyam . . . manyante . . . //"

But nothing of the two
exists for the "fourth" one.

The "shining" one cognizes
neither itself nor others,
neither truth nor lie.
But this "fourth" one
is always the witness
of everything.[21]
(*Māṇḍūkya-kārikā*, 1.11-12)

In Śaṅkara's commentary on the 7th *kārikā* of Gauḍapāda's treatise, where the notion of *turīya* is described at length, it is suggested that all the previous "cosmic" or "perceptive" states are similar to a rope in the hands of a magician: the rope seems to ascend to the skies; however, it is nothing but a trick, which does not fool the more perceptive spectators. Or, as Śaṅkara puts it, "just as a magician remains standing on the ground, being invisible [to the onlookers] due to the veil of his magical illusion, the higher reality, called the "fourth" state, [can only be seen by the Vedānta sages]."[22]

In other words, only this "fourth" state lies beyond duality, beyond the vain and hollow variations of mundane life. In Gauḍapāda's *Kārikās* it is termed a "non-dual" (*advaita*) state. The term "non-duality" is used here to mean both the highest point of the conscious mind and the ultimate reality, identical with liberation. It was due to the emergence of this concept that Gauḍapāda's teaching—as well as the later version of Vedānta, which was developed in Śaṅkara's system—finally came to be

---

21. MK, 1.11-12:

Kāryakāraṇabaddhau tāv iṣyete viśvataijasau /
Prājñaḥ kāraṇabaddhas tu dvau turīye na sidhyataḥ //
Nātmānaṃ na parāṃś caiva na satyaṃ nāpi cānṛtam /
Prājñaḥ kiñcana saṃvetti turyaṃ tat sarvadṛk sadā //

22. Śaṅkara, *Commentary on MK*, 1.7: "sa eva bhūmiṣṭhe māyācchanno 'dṛśyamāna eva sthito yathā tathā turīyākhyaṃ paramārthatattvam /"

known as "Advaita Vedānta," that is, "Vedānta of Non-Duality."

It is tempting to look for the sources of this notion in the Buddhist schools that flourished just before Gauḍapāda came on the scene. A British scholar, F. Whaling, considers it to be historically proven that "Gauḍapāda's Advaita-Vedānta differed from the preceding Vedānta, and many aspects of this difference can only be accounted for if we are ready to accept the fact of a conscious or unconscious borrowing from the theories of Mahāyāna Buddhism."[23] It was probably in the Buddhist Śūnyavāda that Gauḍapāda got his own notion of an opposition between mundane knowledge (*saṃvṛti-satya*) and higher knowledge (*pāramārthika-satya*), as well as his deep belief in the ineffable nature of that higher truth, in its ultimate rejection of all our attempts to have it translated or rendered. Finally, it was undoubtedly Buddhist tradition that first inspired Gauḍapāda to develop the concept of *māyā* or illusion, which he considered to be the foundation of all our worldly knowledge and experience.[24]

Let us see how *māyā* is presented in Gauḍapāda's *Kārikās*. In the passage of the first chapter which immediately follows the indirect description of the "fourth" state,

> When the soul,
> which has been sleeping
> under the influence of endless māyā,
> is [finally] awakened,
> Something unborn, non-dual,
> dreamless and slumberless
> is also awakened.[25]
>
> (*Māṇḍūkya-kārikā*, 1.16)

---

23. F. Whaling, "Śaṅkara and Buddhism," *Journal of Indian Philosophy* 7, no. 1 (1979): 23.

24. The term *māyā* can already be found in *Śvetāśvatara Upanishad* (4.10), where it came to mean the divine creative force, the energy potential of creation (*śakti*), and where it also resembled the concept of *prakṛti*, or primordial matter, the "natural" source of the universe.

25. MK, 1.16:

In other words, we are now dealing with the same kind of opposition found between, respectively, the first three steps on the ladder to a higher reality and the fourth step. Only now it becomes increasingly clear that those first three steps could not take us beyond the limits of illusion, beyond the boundaries of our dreams. The reference point for reality appears only at the apex of the pyramid, and the actual, empirical world, which has presented itself under the guise of stability and solidness, turns out to be nothing but a fleeting illusion. The mist of the dream slowly disperses, the deep slumber dissolves, and now even the ordinary reality of the waking state is suddenly seen from a different angle—it loses all validity. A Buddhist philosopher would probably point out that it is ultimately the "emptiness" (*śūnyatā*), the gaping void, which constitutes not only the lining but the very foundation for every experience, every act of perception. And a staunch Vedāntin, such as Gauḍapāda, is not very far from that outlook when he defends the notion of the illusory character of the empirical universe.

With this perspective, we should go back to the initial interpretation of these four "quarters." It appears decidedly incorrect to imagine them as four segments of one and the same unity or entity. Even the image of a staircase winding upwards or a ladder of existence, even the notion of a gradual ascent, of steps to be taken, seems to be lacking some crucial point. In his commentary on the *Māṇḍūkya-kārikā*, Śaṅkara maintains that it is a far more accurate analogy to imagine each of these "quarters" as respectively smaller denominations of a currency unit. In this way, we can easily see how the smaller, less valuable units of division are subsumed by the higher denominations.[26] These states of consciousness fir into each other somewhat in the manner of *matryoshka* dolls or Chinese

---

Anādimāyayā supto yadā jīvaḥ prabudhyate /
Ajam anidram asvapnam advaitaṃ budhyate tādā //

26. See Śaṅkara, *Commentary on Māṇḍūkya Upanishad*, 2, where the four "quarters," or four "states" of consciousness are likened to the smaller denominations of the Kārṣāpaṇa coin.

boxes, the whole set of which is snugly secured inside the biggest, the most important piece. Similarly, all these "steps," or "quarters," could be regarded as a hierarchical structure, where each higher level completely absorbs and incorporates all the ones below it. In fact, the last verse of the *Māṇḍūkya Upanishad* the interrelation between the "quarters" is established "due to the common measure [with the other states]" (*miteḥ*), as well as "due to the [ability] to swallow up [the preceding states]" (*apīteḥ*).[27]

Now, I believe, the concept of reality in Gauḍapāda's system becomes a bit more coherent. According to it, the highest, the most important state of consciousness is at the same time something like a support, a foundation, an intricate, built-in construction which provides stability to the whole structure of the universe. In Gauḍapāda's words, it is the one and only "reality," which supports everything else. This "fourth" state, which initially seems so elusive and tricky, effectively prevents all other entities from dissolving into a void; without this state, the world would desintegrate into mere nothingness. That

---

27. See *Māṇḍūkya Upanishad*, 11—"the Conscious one, whose state is deep sleep, is the third part [of the Oṃ syllable, namely,] the letter 'm', due to the common measure [with other states] and due to the [ability] to swallow up [the preceding states]"—"suṣuptasthānaḥ prājño makāras tṛtīyā mātrā miter apīter vā . . . /" And the same kind of argument is further developed by Gauḍapāda himself (MK, 1.21):

The "Conscious" one
is established as being identical
with the essence
of the letter 'm',
Since both of them
provide a common measure
[for all other states]
and both are equally capable
of swallowing up
[the preceding states].

Makārabhāve prājñasya mānasāmānyam utkaṭam /
Mātrāsaṃpratipattau tu layasāmānyam eva ca //

is why in the fourth and final chapter of his *Māṇḍūkya-kārikā* Gauḍapāda becomes even more explicit, insisting upon the reality, the eternity and "unborn" nature of this verily ultimate state of consciousness:

> Seemingly born,
> seemingly moving,
> as well as seemingly elemental
> [in its nature]
> Is this consciousness,
> which is unborn,
> immovable and non-elemental.
> [This consciousness] is calm
> and non-dual.[28]
>
> (*Māṇḍūkya-kārikā*, 4.45)

So we can see how, on the one hand, Gauḍapāda apparently sympathizes with a quasi-Buddhist, Yogācāra-like doubt about the reality of the phenomenal universe, while, on the other hand, he seems to oppose Buddhism, presenting his firm belief in some ontological reality which does exist unconditionally and absolutely. Indeed, one is tempted to draw a conclusion from these somewhat vague premises, directly likening Gauḍapāda's concept of reality with that of Śaṅkara's Vedānta. Then, of course, that "fourth" state of consciousness, which cannot be grasped with the help of ordinary means of perception and reasoning, but is, nevertheless, absolutely real, is presented as the higher Self, as pure *ātman*, identical with Brahman. The text of *Māṇḍūkya-kārikā* certainly gives us ample reasons for introducing this analogy. However, let us not jump too soon to these conclusions. Let us try and see whether perhaps some other explanation might prove more apt and coherent.

---

28. MK, 4.45:

Jātyābhāsaṃ calābhāsaṃ vastvābhāsaṃ tathaiva ca /
Ajācalam avastutvaṃ vijñānaṃ śāntam advayam //

In the first chapter of his *Kārikās*, Gauḍapāda suggests a way of approaching that higher reality—a way which is based mainly on special means of meditation, as well as on the use of specially selected sacred chants or incantations (*mantra*). For instance, the four above-mentioned "steps" are reflected in the recitation of the sacred syllable *Oṃ*. Each of the first three states of consciousness is associated with one of the sounds that constitute this syllable according to the rules of Sanskrit phonetics: since the sound *o* is regarded as a diphthong, we get the sound sequence of *a*, *u*, *m*. As Gauḍapāda puts it,

> The sound of 'a'
> leads to the "Universal" one,
> while the sound of 'u'
> leads to the "Shining" one,
> And the sound of 'm'
> leads to the "Conscious" one . . .[29]
> (*Māṇḍūkya-kārikā*, 1.23)

It is interesting to note that the state of *turīya* has no direct correspondence in the phonetic structure of the syllable; the "fourth" state is symbolized by a "point" or "dot" (*bindu*), which essentially forms a part of a graphical outline of an *anusvara*, that is, a sign of nasalization of the diphthong vowel *o*.[30]

---

29. MK, 1.23:

Akāro nayate viśvam ukāraś cāpi taijasam /
Makāraś ca punaḥ prājñam . . . //

30. *Bindu* signifies, primarily, a "drop," a condensed lump of energy. Since this "dot" provides the necessary nasalization of the vowel in the *Oṃ* syllable, we can also regard it as something that ensures indefinite lengthening, indefinite duration of the resounding syllable (it is owing to that, of course, that *Oṃ* syllable is also termed *praṇava*, or the "reverberating" mantra). In some of the Tāntric treatises (especially those belonging to the tradition of Kashmir Śaivism) *bindu* is also considered to be a point of light which is indispensable for the awakening of the "snake energy" or Kuṇḍalinī. According to various Tāntric and Śāktic cults, *bindu* symbolizes the

Primarily, because of that, Gauḍapāda winds up his description with the following words:

> [W]hile for that,
> which cannot be measured,
> there is no movement at all.[31]
> (*Māṇḍūkya-kārikā*, 1.23)

---

moment of coming together, of erotic union between Śiva and Śakti. It is usually presented as an intermingling of two colours: Śiva is the reflective, steady glow of white light (*prakāśa*), and Śakti is the tense, straining and dynamic flashing up of red (*vimarśa*). This "point" already bears in itself both unity and potential diversity, a potential multiplying, creation. In a Kashmir Śaivite treatise *Netra-tantra* ("The Tantra of the Eye"), which was commented upon by Kṣemarāja, it is put in this way: "And this point came to be known as God [the Creator]"—"sa binduś ceśvaraḥ smṛtaḥ" (*Netra-tantra*, 21.66). In one of the Āgamic texts *bindu* is presented as a derivation of "pure consciousness" (*cin-mātra*), though, of course, "consciousness" here embraces both: the "self-luminous" one (*prakāśa*), as well as the aspect of "dynamic, active awareness" (*vimarśa*):

> This [entity], known as the core essence,
> which is [nothing else but]
> pure consciousness,
> having come into contact with light,
> Having condensed itself
> owing to its desire to emit forth
> [its emanations],
> assumes the state
> of a "dot" (*bindutā*).
>
> Sā tattvasaṃjñā cinmātrā jyotiṣaḥ sannidhes tadā /
> Vicikirṣur ghanībhūtā kvacid abhyeti bindutām //
> (*Prapañca-sāra-tantra*, 1.41)

So, this "dot" of pulsating, radiant light, which simultaneously represents the reverberation of phonic energy, already contains the active urge to emanate forth, to shine through, gradually expanding itself into the whole of the created world.

31. MK, 1.23: "nāmātre vidyate gatiḥ."

"That, which cannot be measured," a "measureless" one (*amātra*) is, of course, the pure *ātman*, or, in this case, the adept (*sādhaka*) himself—the adept who from now on has no use for the "measures of sound" (*mātra*), the adept who has left far behind any sound attributes and definitions—in fact, one who is no longer bound even by the concrete phonetic resonance of the syllable *Oṃ*. At the same time, "that, which cannot be measured" is the "measureless" Brahman (since the pure *ātman*, or higher Brahman, is essentially beyond the sphere of ordinary perception and reasoning, it is not "measured" by the valid means of knowledge).[32] For instance, in the *Māṇḍūkya Upanishad* the first three "steps" taken by consciousness (and, respectively, the first three "articulated," "resounding" elements of the sacred syllable *Oṃ*) are defined precisely by their "commensurability" (*miti*, another derivation of the same verb stem *mā*, "to measure"), as well as by their inherent ability to be "swallowed up" or "embraced" (*apīti*), that is, by their complete absorbtion within the fold of a higher hierarchical level (see *Māṇḍūkyopaniṣad*, 11).

Summing up the correspondence between the four states of consciousness and the four elements or "quarters," of the sacred mantra, Gauḍapāda finally announces:

> The *Oṃ* syllable
> should be known by its quarters;
> there is no doubt
> that measures of sound

---

32. The term *pramāṇa*, or the "valid means of knowledge," is derived from the verb root *mā*, which means "to set measure," "to specify." And three main *pramāṇas*: "sense perception" (*pratyakṣa*), "logical argumentation" (*anumāna*), and "testimony of an authority" (*śabda*) all deal with "measurable phenomena," something which still can be shifted around, compared, likened, or sorted out. The main Advaita concept of "Brahman, devoid of attributes" (*nirguṇa-brahma*) is based on the notion of the essential "incommensurability" (*apramātṛtva*) of this higher Brahman and the rest of worldly phenomena. Brahman (or *ātman*) is something which cannot be "measured."

constitute these quarters.
Having known this *Oṃ* syllable
by its quarters,
one should not think
of anything else.[33]
(*Māṇḍūkya-kārikā*, 1.24)

And somewhat later:

The mind should be attached
to the *Oṃ* syllable,
the *Oṃ* syllable is Brahman
devoid of fear.
For him, who is eternally attached
to the *Oṃ* syllable,
there is no fear whatsoever.[34]
(*Māṇḍūkya-kārikā*, 1.25)

Finally, one should note that both the *Māṇḍūkya Upanishad* and Gauḍapāda's *Māṇḍūkya-kārikā* suggest another correspondence, yet another "foursome" of entities. According to the venerated Vedic tradition, the state of wakefulness (the so-called "universal"—*viśva*—state of consciousness) is readily identified with a certain "cosmic" state of the *ātman*. It is assumed that a "wakeful" cosmic soul, usually referred to as a "universal" being, or as a soul, "[embracing] all human beings" (*vaiśvā-nara*), or simply as God the Creator, "enjoys," that is, perceives external objects (numerous worlds, various cosmic manifestations of the universe that was created by his own conscious effort). (See *Māṇḍūkyopaniṣad*, 9.) One might even

33. MK, 1.24:

Oṃkāraṃ pādaśo vidyāt pādā mātrā na saṃśayaḥ /
Oṃkāraṃ pādaśo jñātvā na kiṃcid api cintayet //

34. MK, 1.25:

Yuñjitā praṇave cetaḥ praṇavo brahma nirbhayam /
Praṇave nityayuktasya na bhayam vidyate kvacit //

get the impression that the author of the Upanishad, together with his echoing commentator, is intent on projecting various mental states of an individual soul upon the background of a mythologically construed pattern of the universe. According to Gauḍapāda's own testimony, and that of his commentators (Śaṅkara and some of the later Vedāntins), the second "quarter," or the second "step" of consciousness, corresponds to the so-called "golden germ," or "golden embryo" (*hiraṇya-garbha*); it is basically the same "cosmic soul," only now it is dreaming, inventing for itself a variety of passing images and illusions. The level of the "conscious" one (*prājña*), that is, the level of *ātman* engrossed in deep sleep, corresponds to the "unmanifested" (*avyakta*) state of the cosmic soul; it is a state which prevails in the intervals between successive cycles of creation. It is only at the highest point that pure *ātman*, as an ontological entity, and the "fourth" state of consciousness, might be regarded as approaching one another or even merging together.

3 *Māṇḍūkya-kārikā:* The Illusory World and the Problem of Creation

The second chapter of Gauḍapāda's *Kārikās* is entitled "The Chapter on Falsity" ("Vaitathya-prakaraṇa"). Here, of course, "falsity" comes to mean "unreality," "invalidness," ontological doubtfulness. Since the postulate of the resemblance and even inner similarity of the first three states of consciousness is already presented, Gauḍapāda immediately starts his reasoning with the comparison of perceptions in dreams and in a wakeful state. Some of the first *kārikās* in this chapter deal mainly with reasons based on common sense, and one has to admit that most of these reasons are somewhat naive. The Advaitin maintains, for example, that the objects perceived in a dream cannot be regarded as really existing, because, if they had any ordinary spatial dimensions, they would not on any account be expected to squeeze "inside" (*antaḥ*) the heads of the perceiving subjects:

> [Discerning] people say:
> all the entities,
> [seen] in a dream,
> are false,
> Since these entities stay inside . . .[35]
> (*Māṇḍūkya-kārikā*, 2.1)

---

35. MK, 2.1:

Vaitathyaṃ sarvabhāvānaṃ svapna āhur manīṣiṇaḥ /
Antaḥsthānāt tu bhāvānām . . . //

The same kinds of "spatial," or "dimensional" arguments are used in order to dismiss the very possibility that these objects perceived in a dream (or their perceiving subject) really move in space, changing their places, means, and ways of movement. A similar procedure of *reductio ad absurdum* is applied when Gauḍapāda is using the arguments about "time": a dreaming person simply does not have enough time to undertake all these motions (apparently, time in a dream goes much more quickly) (see *Māṇḍūkya-kārikā*, 2.2).

Up to now, the main emphasis of consideration has been laid on the ability to distinguish between dreams and wakefulness, which is surely within the scope of reasoning of any ordinary, "commonsensical" person. However, it is at this very moment that Gauḍapāda shifts the angle of his approach, trying to use the same rational arguments in order to demonstrate the essential similarity of all perceptions—whether in dreams or in everyday life:

> . . . In the same way.
> perceptions in a wakeful state
> come to be known as false,
> Just like similar [perceptions]
> in a dream . . .[36]
>
> (*Māṇḍūkya-kārikā*, 2.4)

At this crucial moment one certainly feels a bit cheated: a glaring substitution of the logical argument seems too obvious. Let us, however, try to approach the core of the matter from a different angle. Incidentally, what is the base of all this curious argumentation by the Advaitin? He first sets to his task, fervently defending the reality of spatial and temporal relations, and then, with quite an astonishing simplicity and ease, he proposes to completely disregard this reality. To my

---

36. MK, 2.4:

. . . tasmāj jāgarite smṛtam /
Yathā tatra tathā svapne . . . //

mind, one would be justified in regarding these "spatio-temporal" relations as something on a par with Kantian "reine Formen der Überstand," that is, with specific limits and boundary lines, the specific paradigms and irreducible inherent attributes of our consciousness. If space and time are, in reality, nothing but pure and empty "receptacles" of our perception, they should be regarded as the attributes of that perception itself, and certainly not as the ontological traits of reality. Then even the above-cited "general argument" (in Gauḍapāda's terms, *prasiddhena eva hetunā*, that is, "owing to the well-known general argument") becomes entirely plausible and valid; after all, the dreaming state and the state of wakefulness share a common denominator—their main distinguishing attribute is that they are both experienced by us within the ordinary paradigms of perception.

Trying to solve the problem of the ontological nature of the universe, as well as that of its creation, the Advaitin attempts to appreciate the ideas of other schools. For instance, in the fourth chapter of his *Kārikās*, in the chapter where he returns to some of the problems that were posed and analysed before (some of its *kārikās* even supply us with textual repetitions of the verses from the earlier chapters), Gauḍapāda addresses the different versions of the philosophical interpretation of causality.

It is well known that Indian tradition offers two principal approaches to this problem. According to the first one (which was later to be distinguished as *satkārya-vāda*, or "the teaching about the reality of the effect"), any effect really pre-exists in its cause in an involved, latent state. Then any creation (including the creation of the world) is presented as a gradual process of unfolding, of manifestation—a process which is naturally rooted in the cause itself. From the point of view of the second approach (known as *asatkārya-vāda*, or "the teaching about the non-reality of effect"), an effect is born suddenly; it is always a sudden breakthrough, always an interruption, a break of continuity, and therefore an effect is regarded as something absolutely new, as something cardinally different from its own cause.

The first version of causality was mainly advocated by Sāṃkhya. So, the world in this sytem is regarded as a gradual emergence and evolution of the primary "matter" or *prakṛti*. Since *prakṛti* itself is irreducibly real, its own reality is transferred to all its modifications: the objects of the external world are real, because they are all ultimately knitted from the same "threads," or *guṇas*, from the same original "texture" of *prakṛti*. The second approach to causality is more readily associated with Nyāya and Vaiśeṣika—the systems that insist on the emergence of new objects and phenomena out of nonbeing.

Gauḍapāda points out that if one were to accept the position of Sāṃkhya, one would inevitably be confronted with the problem of an infinite regress (*anavasthā*) of the causal chain. An insentient, unconscious cause, which for ever and ever senselessly produces effects, can only lead us astray and destroy any hope for liberation. Besides, as Gauḍapāda emphasizes (and here he is supported by a venerable tradition of Indian philosophy), nothing that is divided or diversified can ever be considered eternal. Moreover, this primordial matter, which is constantly being modified, cannot be regarded as unborn or as something essentially devoid of a beginning. Indeed, the manifoldness and variability associated with this gradual emergence lead us along this line of infinite regress, and the line is endless in both directions. Thus, one cannot hope to determine a point which constitutes a source of all this diversity, any more than one can determine a point where such a diversity might come to an end.[37]

However, since Naiyāyikas' and Vaiśeṣikas' belief in the

---

37. In Gauḍapāda's words,

According to somebody who maintains
  that the cause is the effect,
  the cause itself undergoes birth.
But how can something that undergoes birth
  be regarded as unborn?
  And how can something divided
  be regarded as eternal?

essential difference between a cause and an effect eventually leads them to accept an accidental, unexplained, and sporadic process of creation, their respective systems do not support Gauḍapāda when he is trying to define the ontological status of the world.

The only doctrine that is relatively free of inherent contradictions is, according to Gauḍapāda, the theory of *ajāti* ("absence of origination"), that is, the theory that there was no creation at all. In this view, as soon as we start to reason systematically, we cannot help admitting that the creation of the world, as well as its present existence, are both illusory. As a result, it becomes increasingly easy to equate the waking state to the dream state. Thus, our perceptions when awake are akin to dreams and illusions; they correspond to nothing and only serve as "empty" signs for the invented but ultimately absent objects.

Hence, one of the main tenets in Gauḍapāda's reasoning:

> Something that does not exist
> either in the beginning
> or in the end,
> also does not exist in the present.[38]
> (*Māṇḍūkya-kārikā*, 2.6)

Here we return to the postulates that underlie the Advaita worldview. No entity which has a beginning and an end, no entity which is known as unstable, variable, fluid, ought to be regarded as valid; the only justified conclusion is that it does not exist at all. Everything divided, everything undergoing change, harbours the seeds of its own destruction. Whatever is

---

> Kāraṇaṃ yasya vai kāryaṃ kāraṇaṃ tasya jāyate /
> Jāyamānaṃ katham ajaṃ bhinnaṃ nityaṃ kathaṃ ca tat //
> (*Māṇḍūkya-kārikā*, 4.11)

Even though he does not mention the followers of Sāṃkhya, the argument here is clearly directed against them.

38. MK, 2.6: "Ādāv ante ca yan nāsti vartamāne 'pi tat tathā."

constructed will be destroyed; whatever is emerging, is right from the start contaminated and sick with its own death. Only something that stays forever without change or modification can be termed a "really existing" entity. Therefore, all the entities and objects of perception (whether they are ordinary perceptions of a wakeful and rational subject, or merely fleeting dreams and mirages) are said to be unreal, "false" (*vitatha*, "not so," "unreal"; hence, *vaitathya*); they are false and invalid for the simle reason that they are capable of change. They are in the highest sense of the word "changelings," something akin to "werewolves," something essentially "non-true," deceptively and fearfully illusive.

Moreover, the Advaitin clearly refers us to the Buddhist experience, to the Buddhist world outlook, in which all ordinary mundane phenomena are considered to be "momentary" (*kṣāṇika*, from the word *kṣaṇa*, a "moment"), while the universe is presented as an uninterrupted flow of becoming (the usual Buddhist term is *saṃtāna* or "stream"). On the other hand, even in the *kārikā*, where Gauḍapāda is so keen on justifying the "falsity" of every existing phenomenon, one can easily recognize his ultimate longing for something stable, for some firm and immovable support. And this primordial foundation can be nothing else but the eternal Brahman, which bestows even the passing moments with a tiny share of its own reality, so that they, too, can participate in its eternity.

In Gauḍapāda's words,

> Even in the waking state
> all activity
> perceived by the internal mind,
> should be regarded as unreal,
> Everything that is grasped
> by the external perception,
> [is regarded as] real.
> But it is logically consistent [to assume]
> that, [whatever is grasped]
> in both kinds of perception,

is [essentially] false.[39]

(*Māṇḍūkya-kārikā*, 2.10)

And later, in the same chapter, Gauḍapāda says:

Just as something is seen
in a dream or in an illusion,
just like a magic city of gandharvas
is seen in the sky,—
Just like that the whole universe is seen
by the wise ones,
by those who are well-versed
in Vedānta.[40]

(*Māṇḍūkya-kārikā*, 2.31)

It is interesting to note that this last *kārikā* is lifted almost verbatim from a famous Buddhist text, namely, from Nāgārjuna's *Mādhyamaka-kārikā*, where it is presented in a slightly different form:

Just like an illusion,
just like a dream,
just like a magic city of gandharvas,
Just like [an appearance] of an emergence,—
just like all that,
this state,
this stream [of existence]
is said [to be seen].[41]

(Nāgārjuna, *Mādhyamaka-kārikā*, 7.34)

---

39. MK, 2.10:

Jāgradvṛttāv api tv antaś cetasā kalpitaṃ tv asat /
Bahiś cetogṛhītaṃ sad yuktaṃ vaitathyam etayoḥ //

40. MK, 2.31:

Svapnamāye yathā dṛṣṭe gandharvanagaraṃ yathā /
Tathā viśvam idaṃ dṛṣṭaṃ vedānteṣu vicakṣaṇaiḥ //

41. Nāgārjuna, *Mādhyamaka-kārikā*, 7.34:

One can readily see that in both cases the changeability, the fluidity of existence, is equated with its illusory status. If something flows, changes, and diversifies (and all our perceptions are undoubtedly of this nature, as are their objects, i.e. the manifold phenomena of external world), it is immediately judged as untrue and illusory—just as illusory as the city of heavenly musicians, the Gandharvas, which a fleeting dream sometimes presents to us in the vast empty space of the sky. External objects are unreal, "false" (*vaitathya*), since they can be totally and without any residue reduced to internal perceptions. Because of that it would be much more "economical"—as if making use of Occam's razor and his refusal to multiply unnecessary entities—to bestow reality only upon the perceptions themselves. However, we have an even more valid reason for considering external objects unreal (*asat*), "false," and untrue: they are essentially transient and changing.

But we should not follow these analogies too far. There is, certainly, a crucial difference between the Buddhist approach to the illusory reality of the universe and the Advaitin one. If a Buddhist thinker is mainly concerned about the overwhelming falsity of all natural phenomena, when he opts for a vanishing, dissolving reality, turned into a string of moments that come out of nothingness and return to it, a Vedānta philosopher is looking for a secure and stable support which could hold together the flux of existing phenomena. I would rather say that Gauḍapāda—just like his later follower Śaṅkara—regards a cosmic illusion, *māyā*, more as a veil that covers and conceals the higher reality than as a means to negate it. For both of these Vedāntins, *māyā* is understood primarily in terms of the famous Vedic metaphor of a "hidden," "deeply concealed" (*gūḍha*) Brahman.[42]

Hence, while continuing the same idea, we find a pas-

Yathā māyā yathā svapno gandharvanagaraṃ yathā /
Yathotpādas tathā sthānaṃ tathā bhaṅga udiritaḥ //

42. In this respect one is reminded of the passage from *Kaṭha Upanishad* (*Kaṭhopaniṣad*, 1.3.12):

sage in *Māṇḍūkya-kārikā* which could hardly be envisaged in a purely Buddhist context:

But if in both of these states
    one [readily perceives]
    the falsity of all existing things,
Then who comes to know
    these existing things,
    and who, indeed,
    imagines them?[43]

(*Māṇḍūkya-kārikā*, 2.11)

The answer is given in the following *kārikā*:

The Lord *ātman*
    imagines himself
    through his own *māyā*.
It is He who comes to know
    the existing things.
    That is the firm conviction
    of Vedānta [teaching].[44]

(*Māṇḍūkya-kārikā*, 2.12)

He is hidden in all beings,
    [and because of that]
    he does not shine forth as *ātman*.
However, owing to an astute
    and minute discerning,
    he is seen by those,
    who see minute [things].

Eṣa sarveṣu bhūteṣu gūḍho ''tmā na prakāśate /
Dṛśyate tv agryayā buddhyā sūkṣmayā sūkṣmadarśibhiḥ //

43. MK, 2.11:

Ubhayor api vaitathyaṃ bhāvānāṃ sthānayor yadi /
Ka etān budhyate bhāvan ko vai tesāṃ vikalpakaḥ //

44. MK, 2.12:

Kalpayaty ātmanā ''tmānam ātmā devaḥ svamāyayā /

And somewhat later Gauḍapāda explains the sequence of that "constructing" or "imagining" (*kalpanā*)[45] of existing things. According to the Vedāntin, at first the higher *ātman* creates the illusory idea of an individual soul (*jīva*), and only later, in an effort of creative imagination, it projects the images of external objects and various worldly phenomena; the *ātman* projects the illusory modes of action, as well the equally illusory "fruits" (*phala*) of those actions, all of which are harvested within cycle of saṃsāric reincarnations. The outline of this projection is mapped inside the same pyramidal construction of the states of consciousness; the only difference is that the direction, the vector of the development is exchanged for the opposite one. While an adept who is longing for the ultimate unity with the *ātman* starts his movement with the ordinary waking states of consciousness, imagining himself to be engrossed in manipulations with real external objects, the higher *ātman*, engaged in this play of "constructing" or "imagining," moves from the pure illusions and dreams towards the images of things and phenomena of the empirical world. Later we are going to see whether we are actually dealing here with two different and opposite movements: it is really quite a complicated matter. Let us return now to the passage of Gauḍapāda's text where he discusses the creative activity of the higher *ātman*:

> First of all he imagines
> an individual soul,

Sa eva budhyate bhāvān iti vedāntaniścayaḥ //

45. The word *kalpanā*, which is used in this context, is derived from the verb root *kḷp* (or *vikḷp*), that is, "to imagine," "to produce a mental construction," "to think out." So, the higher Brahman himself, when he is presented as the Lord (*deva*, or, indeed, *īśvara*) assumes the functions of an architect or designer who conceives of a mental, imaginary model, a form of blue-print for the creation of a universe. We shall try to determine later whether for Gauḍapāda (and, for that matter, also for Bhartṛhari) there can be any difference at all between supplying a mental construction and real creation.

and only after that—
[all] existing things,
[taking them] separately, one by one,
Both external and internal ones.
And whatever be the knowledge
[of a soul]—
so is its memory.[46]
(*Māṇḍūkya-kārikā*, 2.16)

So, according to the picture presented by the *Māṇḍūkya-kārikā*, the world of individual souls and external objects is ultimately nothing but the projection of a sole and undivided consciousness. In various passages of his *Kārikās* Gauḍapāda gives this consciousness different names: sometimes it is spoken of as the *ātman* of the Upanishads, sometimes it can be assigned a quasi-Buddhist term (*citta*, or "consciousness," "thought," "mental activity"). The latter term, I believe, really drifted into Gauḍapāda's writings straight from the Buddhist texts. However, one should not forget that while the Buddhist *citta* is essentially momentary and changing, Gauḍapāda tries to preserve the image of the eternal consciousness as that of a stable foundation, underlying the transitory phenomena of the perceived universe. It is often directly identified with the immovable, everlasting and pure *ātman*.

Speaking about the deep abyss which separates the illusory world from the eternal *ātman*, Gaudapada refers us back to the concept that the *ātman* can be conceived both together with the objects as well as separately, independent of them. Yet the objects themselves are only perceived because of the *ātman*; in other words, they are "given" to us only so far as they are clarified by the light of consciousness. Indeed, the *ātman* can exist without any objects. Meanwhile the objects are deficient in their reality, they are not entirely whole—they exist because of

---

46. MK, 2.16:

Jīvaṃ kalpayate pūrvaṃ tato bhāvān pṛthag vidhān /
Bāhyān ādhyātmikāṃś caiva yathā vidyās tathā smṛtiḥ //

the reflected light of the *ātman*. As Gauḍapāda puts it,

> This [*ātman*] is posited
> together with unreal existing things,
> but it can also be posited
> without them.
> The existing things, however,
> are [invariably] posited
> together with this non-dual [*ātman*];
> that is why non-duality
> is so auspicious.[47]
> (*Māṇḍūkya-kārikā*, 2.33)

Thus, while choosing between the two aspects of *ātman* (and, for that matter, between the two aspects of being in general), one should always opt for the "non-dual" (*advaita*) one. Or, to reiterate it in Gauḍapāda's own words,

> And therefore, having known it so,
> one has to confirm one's memory
> in non-duality.[48]
> (*Māṇḍūkya-kārikā*, 2.36)

And it is from this starting point that Gauḍapāda proceeds to construct a peculiar hierarchy of levels of being, together with a corresponding hierarchy of their respective perceptions. Although the first three states of consciousness, as well as the phenomenal world which is revealed in them, are considered to be only relatively, incompletely and illusively real, they cannot by simply labelled as accidental mistakes and flaws. Rather, one derives from them an impression of the true reality which

---

47. MK, 2.33:

Bhāvair asadbhir evāyam advayena ca kalpitaḥ /
Bhāvā apy advayenaiva tasmād advayatā śivā //

48. MK, 2.36:

Tasmād evaṃ viditvainam advaite yojayet smṛtim /

is eventually reflected (or refracted) in these states in a multitude of different ways. The impression is that of the light of consciousness which becomes weaker and dimmer as it travels further from the initial point of absolute non-duality. The picture is somewhat akin to the theoretical notions of Neoplatonism, where the primordial light grows less and less bright, until it becomes almost totally extinguished, being refracted and ultimately swallowed up within the layers of inert matter.

Of course, the origins of this notion of Gauḍapāda can be traced back to the Buddhist theory of "two truths," with its opposition between "vain," "mundane," "hidden" truth (*saṃvṛti-satya*) and absolute, unconditional truth (*paramārtha-satya*). A similar notion concerning the hierarchy of being and knowledge constitutes one of the main theoretical postulates of Śaṅkara's Advaita Vedānta. The latter philosopher, for instance, was keen on distinguishing between "empirical," "unreal," or "pragmatically valid" knowledge (*vyāvahārika-jñāna*), and its counterpart, "the higher," or "the absolute" knowledge, the knowledge "from the standpoint of absolute truth" (*pāramārthika-jñāna*).

It is quite appropriate to regard Gauḍapāda's teaching as a possible variation on the same theme of universal hierarchy, where each successive "level," or "step" (*pāda*) becomes increasingly more real, taking its own place within the hierarchical structure of being. However, we are dealing here with a more complicated case. To my mind, these four states of consciousness, as well as their corresponding four cosmic aspects of the Godhead, and the four "steps" taken towards ultimate liberation, are different in their essence from the envisaged multilayered structure of the universe. I believe all of them are much more closely and directly related to the initial pure consciousness.

In his book on Gauḍapāda, Colin A. Cole writes about the meditation on Brahman: "The method of 'Asparśa Yoga' can be called the 'non-mind technique' for its task is to render the mind quiescent or motionless (*anagama*). Mind in the form of the experience of empirical consciousness is to be transformed into its real nature as pure non-dual consciousness."[49] One might, to some extent, agree with these definitions (though, in general, the idea of "motionlessness" does not greatly appeal to me in the context of Gauḍapāda's teaching). But several pages later the scholar explains that in his opinion the main difference between the system of Gauḍapāda and earlier versions of Vedāntic thought lies in Gauḍapāda's pronounced preference for "much more profound meditative tasks" than those set for a mantra-biased adept.[50] I do not believe in praising a religious philosopher just because he allegedly thinks "more deeply," or "more profoundly," or even "more abstractly." If we wish to grasp Gauḍapāda's unique place in the history of religious thought, we would do better to concentrate on specific traits of his concept of consciousness—consciousness, which for him is ultimately equated with eternal salvation.

It is true that in essence Gauḍapāda does not differ from Śaṅkara in his concept of salvation. Indeed, in contrast to the Buddhist doctrine, the liberation (*mokṣa*) from the saṃsāric cycle of rebirths is regarded by him as "the achievement (or "realization") of something already achieved" (*prāptasya prāpti*), since this liberation (unlike Buddhist *nirvāṇa*) is not something to be attained simply by the efforts of an adept: liberation itself, being initially identical with pure *ātman*, is inherent in the world itself, lending support and reality both to this world and to the efforts of somebody aspiring for liberation. "The realization of something already realized" actually means the return of an individual soul to its own essence, and precisely because of that it is treated not as an action but as a special kind of knowledge or revelation. While we are still moving forward on our way towards liberation, we are by no means engaged in creating Brahman out of our own strivings or

49. See Cole, *Asparśa-yoga*, 111-12.

50. "Meditation on the Self, being neither a point nor an object but the existential subject, thus appears to be a difficult task as it is quite unlike a technique involving concentration on some object which the subjective mind may grasp"—Cole, *Asparśa-yoga*, 114.

wishes. Rather, we are only getting to know something which always existed, something which is undoubtedly much more real than the imaginations or attributes of our own soul. As Gauḍapāda tries to explain it,

> It is maintained
> that this unborn knowledge,
> devoid of mental constructions,
> is not different
> from the [objects] to be known.
> [Meanwhile,] Brahman as something to be known
> is eternal.
> Unborn *ātman* [can be known]
> only through the equally unborn
> [knowledge].[51]
>
> (*Māṇḍūkya-kārikā*, 3.33)

---

51. MK, 3.33:

Akalpakam ajaṃ jñānaṃ jñeyābhinnaṃ pracakṣate /
Brahmajñeyam ajaṃ nityam ajenājam vibudhyate //

4 *Māṇḍūkya-kārikā*: The Shimmering of Cosmos

We should now briefly return to the fourfold structure of consciousness and the universe presented by Gauḍapāda. Actually, one can name several structures like that if one analyzes the text of the *Māṇḍūkya-kārikā*. There are, of course, the four successive "steps" (*pāda*), the four "aspects" of the cosmic soul, as well as the four phonetic elements of the sacred syllable *Oṃ*. And we might recall other foursomes as well: in the third chapter of his *Kārikās* Gauḍapāda mentions the first three "stages of life," or *āśramas* (even though the fourth one is not named, it is clearly implied),[52] and the four "envelopes" or "sheaths" (*kośa*) of *ātman*.[53] One could even take into account the very text of the *Māṇḍūkya-kārikā* itself, which is conveniently divided into four chapters; the fourth chapter is clearly set apart from all the rest owing to its lexical peculiarities, while the first three are, to some extent, embraced by it. In fact, the fourth chapter even refers to the preceding ones directly and repeats whole passages verbatim from the previous text.

How are we supposed to deal with all these fourfold structures? After all, if what we really encounter here are serial sets composed of different elements, then we are facing a dilemma: either there are far too many of these sets, or most of them are nothing but a projection of the "main" or "basic" structure. One can easily devise a chain of reasoning based on the

52. See MK, 3.16.

53. See MK, 3.11.

assumption of a special relationship binding together a "microcosm" and a "macrocosm."[54]

Indeed, why should one not regard all these "cosmic," "universal" structures as direct projections of mental structures, as a kind of a curious psychology which came to be projected onto the structures of the universe? Or, from an opposite perspective, why should one not consider the analytics of individual consciousness to be nothing in its essence but a somewhat paler reflection of much more universal, crucial aspects of being, a somewhat faded-out shadow of ontological structures?

As soon as we are prepared to take this approach, the intermediate position of Gauḍapāda, suspended somewhere half-way between Buddhism and Vedānta, can immediately be determined and pinpointed. The important thing here is to decide which of the two aspects one wants to emphasize; but that is, after all, something that can be chosen somewhat arbitrarily, according to the preferences and predispositions of the historian of philosophy. If the accent is placed upon the inner structures of consciousness, Gauḍapāda is shifted in the general direction of the Buddhist schools. If, however, it is the other way round, and one feels more inclined to start with the notion of the eternal *ātman* (with a suitable ontology, which is gradually translated into corresponding cosmological and mythological tenets), Gauḍapāda is conveniently pushed towards traditional, orthodox systems. I must admit that I used a similar enough method myself (naturally, placing my bets with a sec-

54. This kind of approach was used by André Padoux when he was dealing with the main correspondences and correlations of "mental" and "universal" entities within the framework of Śaiva philosophy: "The theory seems to be a transfer on the cosmic plane of psychological observations. Śaiva cosmogony often appears as a "cosmization" of psychological experiences and vice-versa" (A. Padoux, *Vāc*, 78). However, while the approach suggested in his book apparently works quite well for the systems of Kashmir Śaivism (and might probably be successfully implemented for the purpose of explaining the origins of Gauḍapāda's thought), it is hardly exhaustive and consistent enough to account for some of the traits that are clearly present in the ontological context of the *Māṇḍūkya-kārikā*.

ond, "ontological," so to speak, approach) when I was trying to cope with the notions of early Vedānta in my book on Śaṅkara.[55] That is why Gauḍapāda was presented there as a deplorably inconsistent, "immature" Vedāntin who had not yet overcome his earlier Buddhist preferences and lexical tastes.

Now, I believe, this viewpoint is rather fruitless when trying to understand something about Gauḍapāda himself, or when we try to come to terms with his own peculiar notions, his own peculiar way of thinking. What if these recurrent "foursomes" are not rigid structures at all? What if they cannot be regarded as sets of elements, as fixed points on the map of the universe? Is there not a possibility of taking them as a fair indication of an existence and activity of some—as Roland Barthes would term it—"structure-creating process" which is at work? Perhaps, after all, it is not the elements that matter, but the ever-recurring patterns of their emergence?

The "foursomes" are being born over and over again, because the only thing in existence is the presence of the "power lines," the ever-emerging "field of tension," which is always organizing these foursomes in accordance with the same rules. The elements themselves are devoid of a stable ontological status, so that the very question of some of them being more "real" than others becomes futile. The true reality lies in the "field" itself; it lies in the energy "net" (*reseau*, or, better still, *la grille*) which is ever producing its own "knots" and "connections"; it lies in the configuration of the power lines. What is being determined are not the points of the structure but a general outline and a blueprint of their inner correlations.

I suggest we adopt this hypothesis, for it enables us to grasp the curious notion of *spanda* ("vibration," "pulsation," "shimmering"), which is introduced by Gauḍapāda and which otherwise would remain utterly mystifying. The term *spanda* itself suddenly surfaces in the fourth chapter of *Māṇḍūkya-kārikā*, a chapter, as I mentioned above, that is clearly set apart from the rest of the treatise.

---

55. See Natalia Isayeva, *Shankara and Indian Philosophy* (Albany: SUNY Press, 1991), 12-13, 31-38.

The chapter is named "*Alāta-śānti-prakaraṇa*," that is, "The Extinguishing of the Burning Coals." Many scholars have noted that its text is surprisingly close to the works of the earlier Buddhist philosophers Nāgārjuna (2nd century A.D.) and Asaṅga (4th century). Of course, most of this impression of similarity is due to the occurrence of a special term used in this chapter for the designation of consciousness. Instead of words like *jñana* or *vijñana*, quite appropriate for a Vedāntin (especially, when these words are used to convey the meaning of pure consciousness, or *ātman*), Gauḍapāda is prone to use *citta*, which seems to be directly borrowed from the Buddhist texts.

In his commentary on the *Māṇḍūkya-kārikā*, Śaṅkara writes that although his teacher Gauḍapāda occasionally assumes the standpoint of the Vijñānavāda Buddhists, the main reason for such an unorthodox approach is to demonstrate the absurdity and fallacy of the Buddhists, who refuse to recognize the reality of the external world.[56] Quite in tune with this venerated Vedānta tradition, a present-day Indologist, T. M. P. Mahadevan maintains that Gauḍapāda made use of the whole scope of the Buddhists' argumentation and terminology as a kind of excusable trick in order to lure them all the more successfully into the fold of his own orthodox philosophy.[57]

The terminology of the fourth chapter of the *Māṇḍūkya-kārikā* is really surprisingly close to the vocabulary of the Buddhist texts. Since the whole of worldly practice is equated with dreams, it is no wonder that any going beyond its limits should be defined as a "wakening up" (*prabodha*). It is, indeed, worthy of note that the sages who are supposed to have attained liberation (or those who show the right way towards liberation) are called "the awakened ones" (*prabuddha*, or simply, *buddha*).[58] Even the Buddha himself comes to be mentioned in

---

56. See Śaṅkara, *Commentary on the "Māṇḍūkya-kārikā,"* 4.27.

57. See T. M. P. Mahadevan, *Gauḍapāda: A Study in Early Advaita* (Madras, 1952), 239.

58. Some of the present-day scholars who sympathize with

Gauḍapāda's text,[59] though Śaṅkara in his commentary hastens to explain that while the Buddha actually succeeded in approaching non-duality, still "the real non-duality, the essential nature of the higher being, is only known through to the Upanishads."

The very division of knowledge into three types—"dual worldly" (*dvayam laukikam*), "pure worldly" (*śuddham laukikam*), and "over-worldly" (*lokottaram*)—is an almost literal reiteration of the division suggested in the *Laṅkāvatara-sūtra.*[60] However, if one were to judge from the context of the fourth chapter of the *Māṇḍūkya-kārikā*, all these three kinds of knowledge correspond to the above-mentioned relationship between the "waking" state (*jāgarita*), the "dreaming" state (*svapna*), and the state of "deep sleep" (*supta*). In Gauḍapāda's words,

---

Buddhism, in particular, V. Bhattacharya, tend to identify Gauḍapāda's "yoga free from contacts," or "intangible yoga" (*asparśa yoga*) with the ninth *dhyāna* of the Buddhists. And Śrīharṣa, an Advaitin who lived in the twelfth century, could well write in his work *Khaṇḍana-khaṇḍa-khādya* ("The Assimilation of the Chapters on Refutation") that he has nothing to say against the Mādhyamaka philosophers, since, in his opinion, the Buddhist school of Śūnyavāda is very close to Advaita tenets (see Phyllis Granoff, *Philosophy and Argument in Late Vedānta: Śrī Harsha's Khaṇḍana-khaṇḍa-khādya* [Dordrecht-Boston-London, 1978]). Paul Hacker, undoubtedly one of the finest religious scholars, shared this wide-spread belief in the Buddhist tendencies of Gauḍapāda (and, incidentally, of "early" Śaṅkara as well). One could cite in this respect a well-known work: P. Hacker, *Śaṅkara der Yogin und Sankara der Advaitin. Einige Beobachtungen.—Beiträge zur Geistesgeschichte Indiens.* Festschrift fur Erich Frauwallner, herausgegeben von G. Oberhammer (Vienna, 1968).

59. See *Māṇḍūkya-kārikā*, 4.99.

60. See *Laṅkāvatara-sūtra*, 3.156-57:

O mahamati, there exist three kinds of knowledge: the "worldly" (*laukika*) one, the "over-worldly" (*lokottara*) one, as well as the "super-worldly" (*lokottaratāma*) one. The "worldly"

The "dual worldly" state
is considered to be given to us
together with objects
and together with perception.
The "pure worldly" state
is considered to be given
without objects
but together with perception.
The "over-worldly" state
is traditionally believed to be given
without objects,
and without perception.
However, there [still] exist
both the knowledge
and its object . . .[61]
(*Māṇḍūkya-kārikā*, 4.87-88)

---

knowledge is characteristic of fools, immature [thinkers] and all those [allegedly] wise who persist in defending [the duality] of being and non-being. The "over-worldly" knowledge is characteristic of all the śravakas and pratyeka-buddhas who persist in defending [the dual division] of a particular and a whole. The "super-worldly" knowledge is characteristic of the buddhas and the bodhisattvas, it is free from [the duality] of being and non-being, since it is derived from the seeing of [something] devoid of emergence and destruction.

Tatra mahāmate triprakāraṃ jñānaṃ laukikaṃ lokottaraṃ ca lokottaratāmamṃ ca / tatra laukikaṃ jñānaṃ sadasat pakṣābhiniviṣṭānāṃ sarvatīrthakārabālapṛthagjanānāṃ ca / tatra lokottaraṃ jñānaṃ sarvaśravakapratyekabuddhānāṃ ca svasāmānyalakṣaṇapātītaśayābhiniviṣṭānām / tatra lokottaratāmamṃ jñānaṃ buddhabodhisattvānāṃ nirābhāsa . . . anirodhānutpādadarśanāt sadasatpakṣavigatam . . . pravartate /

61. MK, 4.87-88:

Savastu sopalambhaṃ ca dvayaṃ laukikam iṣyate /
Avastu sopalambhaṃ ca śuddhaṃ laukikam iṣyate //
Avastv anupalambhaṃ ca lokottaram iti smṛtam /
Jñānaṃ jñeyaṃ ca . . . //

It is interesting that we actually get here also, right in the second part of the 88th kārikā, the missing fourth element—it is presented in the guise of a "goal of knowledge," or of "something to be known" (*vijñeyam*), which corresponds to the pure, ultimate state of consciousness. In other words, we get the same fourfold structure, where *vijñeyam* takes the place of the *turīya* consciousness; that is, it stands here to denote the state of knowledge, which is presumed to be totally devoid of the ordinary manifold diversity of its forms and means.

What is the image of this "fourth," pure state of consciousness presented in the last chapter of the *Māṇḍūkya-kārikā*? Gauḍapāda suggests that of a burning fire-brand which is almost extinguished but still smouldering, so that it is intermittently shining forth and dying out:

> Just as the smouldering of a fire-brand
> might appear [to us]
> as even or interrupted,
> and so on,
> The vibration of consciousness
> appears as if divided
> between perception itself
> and [the one] who perceives.[62]
> (*Māṇḍūkya-kārikā*, 4.47)

So, primarily, consciousness is free from any split into a subject and an object; it is free from any diminishing mutual opposition of the parts involved in this process. And this is to be expected since the fourth "step" (*pāda*) taken by consciousness must necessarily embrace and absorb all of the preceding states, integrating and cancelling all their attributes. At the same time, this consciousness can take the form of a "vibration," "pulsation," "shimmering" (*spanditā*)—that is, a kind of wave or energy field, which becomes activated due to its

62. MK, 4.47:

Rjuvakradikābhāsam alātaspanditaṃ yathā /
Grahaṇagrāhakābhāsaṃ vijñānaspanditaṃ tathā //

own inner measure of tension.[63] In his commentary on Gauḍapāda's text, Śaṅkara introduces yet another illustration: a fire-brand is whirled in a circle, and the movement is so fast that only the circle of fire can be seen; once can no longer distinguish the separate positions of the torch, the points of its trajectory. The successive positions in space cease to be significant; what is real, what makes sense to us is the glowing whole which is being shaped into a pattern, into a geometrical figure with its own outline and its own meaning. We can read only the pattern; the exact position of the fire-brand becomes irrelevant and illusory.

It seems, then, to be quite proper and natural that the "purification" of consciousness should be equated to the "calming down," the "dying out" of these turbulent waves. The "vibration" has to settle down; once started, once agitated, the illusory ripples of the created universe must subside, must return to their initial latent state. It is there, inside the folded bud, where all the potential drives of becoming are brought to a standstill, that the inherent energy "seed" or "germ" (*bīja*) lies in wait and finds its abode, ready to burst forth in a new universal cycle of creation. And it is because of this peculiar character of becoming that all the apparent reflections, all the beings that ultimately form the created world, cannot be defined either as ontologically real or as totally unreal. As Gaudapāda puts it,

---

63. The nearest analogy from the European cultural tradition is probably the notion of Heraklites' "fire" (πῦρ):

> And this cosmos, being one and the same for everybody, was not created by any gods, was not created by any men; it always was, it is, and it will be the eternally alive fire, which is burning forth at its own measure, and is burning out at its own measure (κόσμον τὸν αὐτὸν ἁπάντων οὔτε τις θεῶν οὔτε ἀνθρώπων ἐποίησεν, ἀλλ᾽ ἦν ἀεὶ καὶ ἔστιν καὶ ἔσται πῦρ ἀείζωον, ἁπτόμενον μέτρα καὶ ἀποσβεννύμενον μέτρα). (Heraklites. Fragm. 51 [30 DK]—see Clement of Alexandria, *Stromaton*, V, 103.6.)

While the fire-brand
is still burning,
those appearances
do not come to it
from anywhere.
Nor do they go away from it
anywhere
after it is extinguished.[64]
(*Māṇḍūkya-kārikā*, 4.49)

This image of a multitude of elements, bursting forth for a second—the elements that just for a moment flash into existence in order to give birth to similar discrete particles—reminds one of the Buddhist teaching of "momentariness" (*kṣaṇika-vāda*). Indeed, it is reminiscent of the picture of the world presented by the Mādhyamikas, where all the existing dharmas are ultimately based upon the void (*śūnya*), where they are brought into being out of this nothingness and come back to be swallowed by it.[65] To some extent that corresponds

---

64. MK, 4.49:

Alāte spandamāne vai nābhāsā anyatobhuvaḥ /
Na tato 'nyatra nispandān nālātaṃ praviśanti te //

65. Compare this with an image derived from an entirely different cultural tradition. Russian absurdist poets of the 1920s and 1930s (namely, Daniil Kharms and Aleksandr Vvedensky) not only engaged in literary experiments, but also dabbled in philosophical theories (which, in itself, does not seem too surprising, since even modest enough exercises in philology and grammar often prove to be directly linked to a new awareness of language, sometimes producing spectacular results in the field of the philosophy of language). In their posthumous papers one can see curious and distorted fragments devoted to the concept of the "shimmering" of the world. This inner "trembling," "pulsation," or "shimmering" (the actual Russian term used is *mertsaniye*) becomes apparent as soon as we demonstrate our intention to go to the ultimate limit of splitting or dividing the texture of the universe. A. Vvedensky used to call the process itself "a nominative reduction," a process based upon a peculiar absurdist

to Gauḍapāda's intuitions, but I think it is important to keep in mind that the Advaitin finds his support and inspiration elsewhere—certainly not in the Buddhist notion of an infinitesimally small unit or limit of division, where the elements of existence gradually lose all their substantiality, turning into evasive and disappearing momentary "qualities" or "attributes." What really remains immovable and stable for Gauḍapāda is the fourfold relationship itself, even though the

---

tenet. One is supposed to follow the running of a mouse, dividing it into a sequence of stages, until we gradually come to the ultimate points, and then suddenly notice that each of them is different from the other (just as every Buddhist *kṣana*, or "moment," is qualitatively different from any other "moment" that might emerge later). In contrast to the famous *aporia* of Zeno, we do not wind up with the complete halting of the movement; what we get, in Vvedensky's opinion, is the very movement itself, which becomes "continuously discontinuous," a movement in which it is now impossible to distinguish the exact locations, the successive positions of the running mouse. The movement which has been dispersed and broken down into its tiniest particles, no longer "belongs" to any particular agent or represents any fixed or real entity; it rather reveals its inner affinity with the throbbing and pulsating universe itself. Or, as a present-day Russian scholar, V. Podoroga, puts it, "the smallest possible units of time cannot be named, they can only gleam. The moments of shimmering are the moments of something new emerging. The moments, or the 'points of time,' are now too different from each other for us to believe that not so long ago they still belonged to the running of that particular mouse" (V. Podoroga, "On the Problem of the Shimmering of the World, *Logos* 4 [1993]). It is interesting to note that Henri Bergson, when he was trying out the same kind of "reduction," mentally splitting time into infinitesimally small units, ultimately reached something akin to the quasi-Buddhist notion, which he named the "moment of becoming," or "duration" (*la durée*). Podoroga, who seems to be more interested in the ideas of Russian absurdist poets, identifies the ultimate limit of the reduction with a moment of "poetical nonsense," with a split second, when language "loses its grip over reality." Or, one could argue, with a split second when, quite on the contrary, language finally assumes its superior power over the world.

pulsating inner links prove to be more essential than the *grille*, and the inner pattern of being is indisputably more permanent than the elements forming this eternal configuration.

I will return presently to the somewhat mystifying recurrent "fourfoldedness" of the pattern. Now let us turn to the "shimmering" or "pulsation" itself. As Gauḍapāda says towards the end of his *Māṇḍūkya-kārikā*,

> This duality,
> similar to [the duality]
> of the perception and the perceiver,
> is only the vibration of consciousness.
> But consciousness is devoid of objects;
> that is why it is called
> eternally free from bonds.[66]
> (*Māṇḍūkya-kārikā*, 4.72)

---

66. MK, 4.72:

Cittaspanditam evedaṃ grāhyagrāhakavad dvayam /
Cittaṃ nirviṣayaṃ nityam asaṅgam tena kīrtitam //

There is a similar passage in a famous treatise of Kashmir Śaivite tradition—Utpaladeva's *Īśvara-pratyabhijñā-kārikā* ("The Kārikās on the Recognition of the Lord") (the first half of the 10th century), commented upon by his disciple Abhinavagupta:

Ātmānam ata evāyaṃ jñeyīkuryāt pṛthak sthiti /
Jñeyaṃ na tu tadainamukhyat khaṇḍyetāsya svatantratā //

Because of this [vibration],
this [pure Self]
makes himself into
an object of knowledge.
But the objects have no
separate existence,
since otherwise
his freedom would be shattered
(Utpaladeva, *Īśvara-pratyabhijñā-kārikā*, 1.15)

The interpretation that suggests "vibration," or *spanda*, is given in Abhinavagupta's commentary, *Pratyabhijñā-kārikā-vimarśinī*.

As it states in the 75th *kārikā* (and then reiterated in the 79th), this "consciousness" (*citta*) initially engages in the vibration due to its "passionate attachment" (*abhiniveśa*) to unreal objects, due to its own strange whim, which forces it to "imagine" all these unreal entities. And every time Gauḍapāda's *Kārikās* mention this consciousness, devoid of attributes and uncreated, every time they introduce the notion of consciousness that in its own supreme effort starts to create (or manifest) the world of phenomena, Śaṅkara, commenting on the *Kārikās*, patiently explains each time that Gauḍapāda is referring to the higher Brahman of the Upanishads. In order to preclude any possibility of a purely psychological interpretation of this passage on the "vibration of consciousness," Śaṅkara is quick to supply us with an appropriate *śruti* verse concerning the higher reality devoid of bonds and relations.[67]

It certainly seems that Gauḍapāda himself would not have rejected this kind of interpretation. After all, for him

> This turns out to be unborn,
> devoid of deep slumber,
> devoid of dreams,
> and self-luminous.
> Since this entity
> is eternally self-effulgent
> by its very nature.[68]
> (*Māṇḍūkya-kārikā*, 4.81)

---

67. We can easily see how Śaṅkara inserts an appropriate saying from the *Bṛhadāraṇyaka Upanishad* into his commentary on the 72nd *kārikā* of the fourth chapter: "He is not touched by anything of what he can see in this state, since this [higher] Man is [by its nature] devoid of any bonds." Sa yat tatra kiṃcit paśyaty ananvāgatas tena bhavati asaṅgo hy ayaṃ puruṣa iti / (*Bṛhadāraṇyakopaniṣad*, 4.3.15). And even though the above-cited passage introduces the notion of a "[higher] Man" (*puruṣa*), that is, the notion of the higher *ātman*, which is devoid of any relations while he is engrossed in the state of a deep sleep, in the following passage of the Upanishad (4.3.16) the same words are repeated concerning the *ātman* that comes back to his ordinary waking state.

68. MK, 4.81:

One should note, incidentally, that in the orthodox philosophical tradition the very word "self-luminious" (*prabhāta*) was a common epithet for the pure consciousness that was identical with the *ātman*. Indeed, this kind of consciousness does not depend on anything else to reveal its own being. The *ātman* does not need the presence of any other consciousness, any other witness to be persuaded of its own existence or reality. Its reality is revealed in a sudden flash, in a sudden outburst of intellectual intuition, which is based upon the immediate perception of "I am." This kind of approach to the nature of the *ātman* helped Advaita to avoid the *regressus ad infinitum* (*anavasthā*) characteristic of Nyāya-Vaiśeṣika schools of reasoning, where the conscious subject was supposed to rely on a different consciousness in order to be able to ascertain his own being. In Advaita there was no need for this infinite line of witnesses: the regress is forcibly stopped and brought to an end as soon as it comes upon the inner consciousness of the subject, upon the perception of himself as a "witness" (*sākṣin*), as a "seer" or "onlooker" (*drāṣṭṛ*), whose gaze always begins its travel from the inside to the outside.[69]

In the words of Gauḍapāda,

Ajam anidram asvapnaṃ prabhātaṃ bhavati svayam /
Akṛd vibhāto hy evaiṣa dharmo dhātusvabhāvataḥ //

69. Note the passage from the *Bṛhadāraṇyaka Upanishad* often cited by Śaṅkara: "It is impossible to see the witness of the seeing . . . and it is impossible to think the thinker of the thought"—"Na dṛṣṭer draṣṭāraṃ paśyeḥ . . . na vijñāter vijñātāraṃ vijānīyāḥ /" (*Bṛhadāraṇyakopaniṣad*, 3.4.2). This problem borders on the similar problem of the self-reflection of consciousness, since, according to Śaṅkara, the pure foundation of consciousness can never turn back on itself in order to grasp its own essence, nor can it ever become its own object: "The action directed towards its own source, cannot be [thought about] without entailing inner contradictions,—indeed, the burning fire cannot burn itself, and the most able actor cannot climb on his own shoulder."—"Tarhi . . . na tad dharmatvam asnuvita svātmāni kriyāvirodhāt / na hy agnir uṣṇaḥ san svātmānaṃ dahati / na

> Owing to his attachment
> to all kinds of objects
> this Lord [*ātman*]
> Is always easily hidden under a veil,
> but is hard to reveal.[70]
> (*Māṇḍūkya-kārikā*, 4.82)

In other words, due to a strange whim (one which is quite understandable), the Lord (*bhagavān*), that is, pure *ātman*, likes to play hide-and-seek, likes to hide his own being under the heap of "imagined," "mentally constructed" entities or names. The motive (or reason) for this becomes clear when we recall a text from the *Bṛhadāraṇyaka Upanishad*: "Since the gods somehow like indirect (*parokṣa*, literally: "far from the eye," "concealed from view") and hate direct (*pratyakṣa*) [naming]" (*Bṛhadāraṇyakopaniṣad*, 4.2.2).[71]

And, finally, the *Māṇḍūkya-kārikā* ends with the praise of some "higher state":

> Having awakened to that state,
> which is inconceivable,
> most deeply hidden, unborn,
> always equal [to itself]

---

hi naṭaḥ śikṣitaḥ san svaskandham adhirokṣyati /" (Śaṅkara, *Commentary on the Brahma-sūtra*, 3.54). It is this kind of consciousness, devoid of any qualities of attributes, which cannot be grasped either by word, concept, or sense image, that becomes totally revealed only in a sudden flash of intuitive perception (*pratibhā*).

70. MK, 4.82:

Sukham āvriyate nityaṃ duḥkhaṃ vivriyate sadā /
Yasya kasya ca dharmasya graheṇa bhagavān asau //

71. "Parokṣapriyā iva hi devāḥ pratyakṣadviṣaḥ /" Concerning the role of an "indirect" definition of *ātman*, as well as the role of the sacred texts in the ontological structure of the universe, see Natalia Isayeva, *Shankara and Indian Philosophy* (Albany: SUNY Press, 1993).

and sacred,
We are praising it
to the best of our abilities.[72]
(*Māṇḍūkya-kārikā*, 4.100)

It is curious that Śaṅkara, who did not grudge any effort to keep the "teacher of his teacher" within the fold of the orthodox tradition, had totally changed the context of the *kārikā* when writing his commentary on it. Trying to avoid unpleasant Buddhist connotations, he substituted Gauḍapāda's usual term of *pādam* ("step" or "state") with the word *brahmanam* ("Brahman"); the replacement neatly fits in the metrical line, coinciding with the initial word even in its grammar form. The verse is paraphrased, the loyalty to the orthodox religion is safeguarded, but this rather arbitrary interpretation entails quite a substantial change of meaning. Meanwhile, Gauḍapāda did not need all this drastic cleansing: in his own way he proved to be as loyal to the Vedic tradition as Śaṅkara himself. He just chose to base his teaching on a different trend of that tradition, a trend as venerated and authoritative as Śaṅkara's own Advaita.

72. MK, 4.100:

Durdarśam atigambhīram ajaṃ sāmyaṃ viśāradam /
Buddhvā padam anānātvaṃ namaskurmo yathābalam //

II Bhartṛhari

Speech and the World: Creation or Expression?

5 Bhartṛhari

Grammar Tradition

Before dealing with Bhartṛhari's system, we should say a few words concerning the place of the grammar theories in Indian philosophical thought. A famous French scholar and expert on Bhartṛhari, Madeleine Biardeau, wrote in her book on the theories of consciousness in Indian grammar tradition:

> [T]he West also has its philosophies of grammar or language, in which grammarians and linguists are prudently suggesting certain limited theoretical notions that seem to be authorized by their own subject. Sometimes these notions boil down to the reshuffling and putting into place the fundamental ideas of their own subject, eventually giving this structure the name of "philosophy." However, being true scholars, they never make any claims to present the total vision of the universe starting from the postulates of their own science—even though secretly they might feel the need to include their particular subject into their concept of the world. On the contrary, we can see, how the Indian thinkers, specializing either in the sacrificial rites, in the logical discussion or in the study of language, not only become theoreticians in their respective domains, but always try to immerse the objects of their own studies into a wider philosophy (taken in the specific sense of the global view of the universe).[1]

---

1. "l'Occident a aussi ses philosophies de la grammaire ou du langage, où grammairiens et linguistes émmettent prudemment les

Meanwhile Indian grammarians were always trying to link purely technical rules and notions with the general structure of the universe, with the notion of the origin of the world and that of its nature. Or, to put it in her own words, we are dealing here with the concept "of the importance of language, which in India (and not only for a grammarian but for all other thinkers as well) becomes not so much an instrument for the expression of thought as a means of knowing the reality and taking possession over it."[2]

This standpoint is to some extent explained by the most general orthodox views on the part played by the sacred texts in the creation and correct maintaining of the universe. One of the more prevalent versions suggests that Brahman, or the higher primordial source, creates the world not in a direct way, but indirectly, starting with the creation of a preliminary matrix, a special kind of pattern, which is eventually followed by the whole structure of the universe. Since time itself, according to the Vedic tradition, is cyclic in its character, every cycle of creation is inevitably followed by the stage of destruction (usually conceived of as a universal fire, *pralaya*, which obliterates all the existing things of the preceding world). The sacred texts play quite a unique part in the course of this oscillation: they

---

conclusions théoriques limitées qui leur semblent autorisées par leur discipline. Parfois même ces derniers se contentent d'une mise en place des concepts fondamentaux de leur science et lui donneront le nom de 'philosophie.' Jamais en tous cas ils ne prétendront donner, en tant que savants, une vision totale de l'univers à partir de leur science, même si pour eux-mêmes ils éprouvent le besoin de replacer leur discipline dans leur conception du monde. À l'inverse, nous voyons les techniciens indiens du sacrifice, de la discussion logique et du langage, non seulement en devenir respectivement les théoriciens, mais englober leur objet d'étude dans une philosophie, au sens specifique de vision globale de l'univers." Madeleine Biardeau, *Théorie de la connaissance et philosophie de la parole dans le brahmanisme classique* (Paris, 1964), 252.

2. "de l'importance du langage qui, pour le grammarien comme pour tous les autres dans l'Inde, est moins un instrument d'expression de la pensée qu'un moyen de connaître le réel et d'avoir prise sur lui." M. Biardeau, *Théorie de la connaissance*, 31.

constitute a peculiar intermediary link between the cycles of creation, ultimately safeguarding the continuity and stability both of the natural and religious laws, as well as the possibility of attaining Brahman and liberation. The very syllables of the Vedas act as a foundation or support both for ordinary natural phenomena (since the latter are organized in coherent and conceivable way), and for human efforts that are made within the sphere of ordinary life, within that of ritual practice, and within the realm of the spiritual knowledge of God.

The whole of Indian grammar theory began with Pāṇini and Yāska (at least, grammar texts preceding their works did not survive to our day). These thinkers lived several centuries before the Christian era, possibly as early as the fifth century B.C.[3] (Incidentally, both of them cite earlier grammarians, in particular, Śākalya, Audumbarāyaṇa, Vārttākṣa, Satakāyana, Gārgya, and others, but none of these works survived up to our day.) Pāṇini's major work is called *Aṣṭādhyāyī* ("The Eight Chapters") and gives a standard analytical description of the Sanskrit language; the first extant comments (*Vārttika*) on Pāṇini's treatise belong to Kātyāyana (probably, the middle of the third century B.C.). However, Kātyāyana's commentaries were preserved only as part of a much later philosophical and linguistical commentary, namely, that of Patañjali.

Patañjali (who is sometimes identified with the great author of the *Yoga-sūtras*) was certainly one of the greatest Indian grammarian-philosophers. He lived about 150 B.C. and presented his ideas in the form of a commentary on Pāṇini's *Sūtras*, as well as in his interpretation (*Vārttika*) of Kātyāyana's comments. Patañjali's commentary on Pāṇini's text, *Mahābhāṣya* ("The Great Commentary"), faithfully follows the sequence of the *Sūtras* of Pāṇini. Actually, the *Mahā-bhāṣya* of Patañjali, and the intense interest he takes in the problem of the eternal status of language and the ability of language to grasp

3. See Harold G. Coward and K. Kunjunni Raja, "Historical Résumé," in Harold G. Coward and K. Kunjunni Raja, eds., *The Philosophy of the Grammarians*, Encyclopedia of Indian Philosophies (Princeton: Princeton University Press, 1990), 13-14.

reality, is wholly consistent with the traditional themes of Indian religious philosophy, where the main emphasis is laid upon the possibility of ultimate liberation from *saṃsāra*, upon the alleged unity of human *ātman* with the higher Brahman, as well as upon the ways of approaching that higher reality. As Harold G. Coward and K. Kunjunni Raja put it, "the goal of the Indian grammarians' philosophy . . . is not mere intellectual knowledge, but direct experience of ultimate truth."[4] Bhartṛhari is said to have written a commentary on this work.[5] Here we are going to deal mainly with an independent treatise by Bhartṛhari, namely, *Vākya-padīya*, the ideas of which loosely correlate with the principal tenets of the grammar philosophy of the earlier stage. Incidentally, there is also an interesting testimonial of two Kashmirian Śaivites, Somānanda and Utpālācārya (about ninth-tenth centuries A.D.), who attribute to Bhartṛhari the authorship of the work *Śabda-dhātu-samīkṣā* ("The Investigation of the Word Roots"), where Bhartṛhari was supposed to deal with the higher form of speech (*paśyantī*); the work itself, unfortunately, was not preserved.[6]

Life and Works of Bhartṛhari

The grammarian Bhartṛhari probably lived around the fifth-sixth centuries A.D. Yet if one relies on the reports of the

4. Harold G. Coward and K. Kunjunni Raja, "Metaphysics," in Coward and K. Kunjunni Raja, *The Philosophy of the Grammarians*, 33.

5. Even the name of this work remains unclear; Indian scholar Ashok Aklujkar points out that most of the references to this commentary on the part of the later grammarians call it *Tri-padī* (["The Work] in Three Parts"). However, the most common name, under which it is mentioned now, is *Mahā-bhāṣya-pradīpikā*, or "Lights on the Great Commentary." Very often it is simply called Bhartṛhari's *Ṭīkā* ("Comment") on *Mahā-bhāṣya*. What is available in manuscript is only a small portion of the work; the rest of it is unfortunately lost.

6. See Ashok Aklujkar, "Bhartṛhari," in Coward and K. Kunjunni Raja, *The Philosophy of the Grammarians*, 122.

Buddhist pilgrim I-Tsing, one must opt for a slightly later date: according to I-Tsing, Bhartṛhari died in A.D. 651.[7] However, Erich Frauwallner and an Indian scholar, H. R. Rangaswamy Iyengar, who found direct borrowings from Bhartṛhari's texts in the works of a Buddhist philosopher Diṅnāga, cannot place the Vedāntist later than the fifth century A.D.[8] A sixth-century Jain philosopher, Siṃhasūrigaṇi, writes that Bhartṛhari studied under the guidance of Vasurāta, who

---

7. See J. Takakusu, *A Record of the Buddhist Religion As Practised in India and the Malay Archipelago* (Oxford, 1896), 180. According to I-Tsing, Bhartṛhari "became seven times a priest and seven times returned to the laity" (Takakusu, *A Record*, 179).

8. See H. R. Rangaswamy Iyengar, "Bhartṛhari and Diṅnāga," *Journal of the Bombay Branch of the Royal Asiatic Society* 26 (1951); E. Frauwallner, "Diṅnāga, sein Werk und seine Entwicklung," *Wiener Zeitschrift für die Kunde Süd- und Ostasiens* 5 (1961): 125. After them it was generally assumed that direct quotations from Bhartṛhari could be found in Diṅnāga's main work, *Pramāṇa-samuccāya-vṛtti* ("The Commentary upon the Collection [of Works] Concerning Valid Means of Knowledge"). The references form a part of the fifth chapter and deal mainly with *apoha-pariccheda* or the "refutation of the exclusion of other [possibilities]" (see S. Katsura, "The Apoha Theory of Dignāga," *Journal of Indian and Buddhist Studies* 28, no. 1 (1979): 16-20. A Japanese scholar, Masaaki Hattori, successfully showed the similarities between Diṅnāga's concept of *apoha* and Bhartṛhari's notion of *jāti* ("general category"), as presented in the second and the third chapters of the latter's treatise *Vākya-padīya* (primarily, in the special section dealing with *jāti*, that is, section 1 of the third chapter) (see M. Hattori, "The Sautrāntika Background of the Apoha Theory," in *Buddhist Thought and Civilization: Essays in Honor of Herbert V. Guenther* (Emeryville, 1977), 50-52). As Harold G. Coward and K. Kunjunni Raja show in their work, Diṅnāga quotes three verses from Bhartṛhari's *Vākya-padīya*, namely, verses 2.155, 2.158, and 3.14.8. Moreover, Diṅnāga finally agrees with Bhartrhari that the meaning of the sentence (*vākya*) can be revealed only in a kind of an "intellectual intuition" (*pratibhā*) (VP, 2.143: "When abstracted from a sentence, the mean-

was distantly related to a pupil of another famous Buddhist thinker, Vasubandhu.[9]

Some historians of Indian culture and literature tend to identify Bhartṛhari the philosopher with the famous Sanskrit poet Bhartṛhari, the author of the three-part verse cycle *Śataka-trayam* ("Three Hundred [Verses]"—the cycle itself embraces *Nīti-śataka* or "A Hundred [Verses] on Moral Law," *Śṛṅgāra-śataka* or "A Hundred [Verses] on Erotical Longing," and *Vairāgya-śataka* or "A Hundred [Verses] on Renunciation"). It is difficult to say whether we are dealing here merely with two contemporaries with the same name, or whether there was actually only one Bhartṛhari—both a thinker and a poet. We can only note that the main philosophical foundations assumed by the author of *Śataka-trayam*, do not contradict the Vedāntic ideas of the philosopher. However, the image of the Vedānta teaching we can get from the poems is a much more generalized one—what is lacking here are probably the peculiarities

---

ing of a word becomes unintelligible. The meaning of a sentence called "intuition" [*pratibhā*] is first produced by this [sentence] itself"—"Apoddhāre padasyāyam vākyād artho vivecitaḥ / Vākyārthaḥ pratibhākhyo yaṃ tenādāv upajanyate //"). (See Shoryu Katsura, "Buddhist Logicians," in Harold G. Coward and K. Kunjunni Raja, *The Philosophy of the Grammarians*, Historical Résumé, 27-28). Basically the same date for Bhartṛhari (fifth century) was also suggested by Hajime Nakamura after a study of Tibetan sources (see Hajime Nakamura, *Tibetan Citations of Bhartṛhari's Verses and the Problem of His Date: Prof. Susumu Yamaguchi Presentation Volume* (Kyoto, 1955), 122-36).

9. Mysore Hiriyanna, *Outlines of Indian Philosophy* (Bombay, 1976), 182-83. E. Frauwallner suggested the following dates: Vasurāta—A.D. 430-490, Bhartṛhari—A.D. 450-510. Bhartṛhari's commentator, Puṇyarāja, mentions Vasurāta several times in his commentary on the second chapter of Bhartṛhari's treatise (*Vākya-padīya*, 2.54, 55, 480, 483). Also, Vasurāta is named as Bhartṛhari's guru by Siṃhasūri in his commentary on Mallavādin's *Naya-cakra* (see K. A. Subramania Iyer, *Bhartṛhari. A Study of the Vākyapadīya in the Light of the Ancient Commentaries* (Poona: Deccan College, 1969), 3.

and distinctive details that attract one to Bhartṛhari's philosophy of grammar. Anyway, these two activities attributed to Bhartṛhari—grammar and moral philosophy—remain, on the whole, separate from one another; and, as K. A. Subramania Iyer puts it in his book on Bhartṛhari, "while the author of *Vākyapadīya* has chiefly been known in grammatical and philosophical circles, the author of these three centuries of poetical stanzas has been far more known among Sanskritists in general."[10]

According to a well-established Indian tradition, in his youth Bhartṛhari went through a short period of infatuation with Buddhist ideas, while later he became a staunch supporter of orthodox Brahmanism. However—and this can be said about many other immediate predecessors of Śaṅkara—Bhartṛhari's teaching sometimes has a distinct Buddhist tinge. Nevertheless, one could still safely place his main work, *Vākya-padīya*, within the fold of Vedānta, though it is certainly far removed from Śaṅkara's Advaita Vedānta. It is interesting to note that Yāmunācārya, in his work *Siddhi-traya*, cites Bhartṛhari as one of the sages who contributed towards the formation of Vedānta.

10. K. A. Subramania Iyer, *Bhartṛhari*, 10-11.

6 *Vākya-padīya*

As it was already said, Bhartṛhari's principal work is his metrical treatise *Vākya-padīya*, that is, "[The Treatise] on the Saying and the Word." It is composed of three chapters (*kaṇḍa*); hence another name by which it became known, *Trikāṇḍī* ("[The Work] in Three Chapters"). The first chapter, "The Chapter on Brahman" ("Brahma-kaṇḍa"), is devoted to the philosophical investigation of the nature of Brahman and the universe. The second chapter ("Vākya-kaṇḍa," or "The Chapter on the Sentence") deals with the sentences that manifest the meaning of a statement, while the third chapter ("Pada-kaṇḍa," or "The Chapter on the Word") deals with the separate words that are brought together to form the sentence. Besides treating purely linguistical matters, the second and the third chapters include discussions on the nature of time, space, the function and origin of general categories, and so forth. Most of the present essay is based on the material of the first chapter of *Vākya-padīya*, which offers the most concentrated exposition of Bhartṛhari's main ideas.

However, before embarking upon this analysis of Bhartṛhari's work, it is important to touch upon a somewhat problematical matter: that of the existing commentaries on *Vākya-padīya*.

The most important of these commentaries is, undoubtedly, *Vṛtti* ("The Interpretation"), often ascribed to Harivṛṣabha. A matter of great controversy among the Indologists taking interest in the philosophy of grammar is the problem of Harivṛṣabha's identity, since he might be Bhartṛhari himself. Indeed, the name 'Harivṛṣabha', just like the name 'Bhartṛhari', literally means "great, powerful Hari," so both of them could be regarded as variations of the same name. The text of the *Vṛtti* was first published in 1934 by Pt. Charudeva Shastri,[11] who regarded it as a part of the *Vākya-padīya* itself, and therefore considered the author of the *Vṛtti* to be Bhartṛhari. Later on, in 1964, the text of the first chapter of the *Vākya-padīya*, accompanied by the *Vṛtti* (together with a French translation) was published by M. Biardeau.[12] In her introduction, the French scholar brought together numerous passages of the most venerated sages of the Indian orthodox tradition (including Kumārila, Helāraja, Maṇḍanamiśra, Abhinavagupta, and others), that indirectly testify to the authorship of Bhartṛhari. Proceeding with her own textual analysis, she was more inclined, however, to regard Bhartṛhari and Harivṛṣabha as two different authors. Meanwhile, in 1969, K. A. Subramania Iyer suggested in his book that one and the same person was the author of both the *Vākya-padīya* and the first two parts of the *Vṛtti*.[13] Ashok Aklujkar, who supplied a chapter on Bhartṛhari for the book *The Philosophy of the Grammarians*, basically holds the same view.[14] Whatever the controversy about the names and the authorship may be, we can safely assume that Bhartṛhari and Harivṛṣabha are similar in their approaches to the entity of the Word (except for a number of passages that can be discussed separately). As Madeleine Biardeau puts it, "Nevertheless, the work of Harivṛṣabha is useful, since it pre-

---

11. Pt. Charu Deva Sastri, *Vākyapadīya with the Commentary of Vṛṣabhadeva* (Lahore: Ram Lal Kapoor Trust, 1934). To be precise, the first excerpts from the *Vṛtti* were published in 1887 by Pt. Gangadhara Sastri Manavalli in the Benares Sanskrit Series, but in this edition the authorship of the commentary was ascribed to Puṇyarāja.

12. M. Biardeau, *Vākyapadīya, Brahmakaṇḍa, avec la Vṛtti de Harivṛṣabha*. Traduction, Introduction et Notes. Publication de l'Institut de Civilisation indienne, fasc. 24. (Paris, 1964).

13. See K. A. Subramania Iyer, *Bhartṛhari*, 16-36.

14. See Ashok Aklujkar, "Bhartṛhari," in Harold G. Coward and K. Kunjunni Raja, *The Philosophy of the Grammarians*, 121.

sents the basic commentary on *Vākya-padīya*, that is, historically, it provides a starting point for every later tentative interpretation of the Kārikās. Devoid of real genius or originality, it still more than once succeeds in clarifying the verse being commented upon, very often putting it in relation with something that Bhartṛhari said in other kaṇḍas."[15] Even if these words seem harsh, they still make it clear that the *Vṛtti* text (at least two of its first kaṇḍas) corresponds to the main notions of Bhartṛhari's *Vākya-padīya*.

One might also mention another famous commentary on the *Vākya-padīya*—the *Prakāśa* ("The [Shining] Light") of Helāraja, a Kashmiri sage, who was allegedly a teacher of Abhinavagupta and lived in the tenth century.[16] Unfortunately, only his commentary on the third chapter of Bhartṛhari's treatise is extant, and so it is in effect beyond the scope of the present work. The same applies to Puṇyarāja's commentary on the second chapter of the *Vākya-padīya*, known under the name of *Parikīrṇa-prakāśa* ("The Light of Explanation").[17]

Anyway, the core ideas of Bhartṛhari's *Vākya-padīya* are outlined right from the start, in the first two *kārikās* of the work:

> Beginningless and endless Brahman—
> that is the essence of the word,
> that is the imperishable [syllable];[18]

---

15. "l'oeuvre de Harivṛṣabha n'en est pas moins utile, ne serait-ce que parce qu'elle forme le commentaire de base du *Vākyapadīya*, c'est-à-dire, historiquement, le point de départ de tout interprétation ultérieure des kārikā. Sans génie, sans originalité, elle éclaire sur plus d'un point les vers qu'elle commente, souvent en les mettant en relation avec ce que B[hartṛhari] a dit dans les autres kaṇḍa." M. Biardeau, *Vākyapadīya, Brahmakaṇḍa*, 21.

16. See S. K. Subramania Iyer, *Bhartṛhari*, 36-40.

17. See ibid., 40-44.

18. "imperishable [syllable]"—*akṣara* (lit., "not fluid," "not flowing," hence "not passing away," "imperishable"). It is also a

It is manifested[19]
in the form of the objects,
it is [something] from which the world
begins to evolve.
It is [taught] by the sacred tradition
to be the One,
yet it is the abode of different powers;[20]
And so, being indivisible,
it nevertheless comes to be divided
owing to these powers.[21]
(*Vākya-padīya*, 1.1-2)

We are eventually going to return to these first *kārikās*. Now it is enough to note some of the terms and expressions that we encounter from the beginning, to help us understand

---

common linguistical term for a distinctive sound unit. M. Biardeau is even prone to call it "le Phonème."

19. "is manifested"—*vivartate*. This is a derivation of the verb stem *vi-vṛt*, that is, "to appear," "to become manifested, apparent." It is one of the most interesting words in Śaṅkara's Advaita Vedānta, where the whole of the universe, the whole of creation is regarded as an "appearance," an "illusion," an "illusory manifestation" (*vivarta*). In Śaṅkara's system *vivarta* initiates quite a long succession of synonymous words which includes *māyā* (illusion), *avidyā* ("ignorance"), *ābhāsa* ("deceptive reflection"), etc.

20. "power"—*śakti* (lit., "potency," "creative force"). In Advaita Vedānta *śakti* is presented not as an independent, autonomous entity, but rather as an energy, totally dependent on Brahman, as Brahman's own creative power. In Śaivism *śakti* is often personified in the form of the independent cosmic "energy" of the supreme Brahman and it is usually presented as a separate goddess, a consort of Śiva.

21. *Vākya-padīya* (hereafter referred to as VP), 1.1-2:

Anādinidhanaṃ brahma śabdatattvaṃ yad akṣaram /
Vivartate 'rthabhāvena prakriyā jagato yataḥ //
Ekam eva yad āmnātam bhinnaśaktivyapāśrayat /
Apṛthaktve 'pi śaktibhyaḥ pṛthaktveneva ca vartate //

some of the peculiarities or apparent discrepancies. Brahman is presented here as the "essence of the word" (*śabda-tattva*)—something which could mean both the hypothetical "initial word" as the source of the universe, and some essential core meaning, deeply engrained in every word being pronounced. Brahman is clearly defined as something "from which the world starts to evolve" (*prakriyā jagato yataḥ*), and this implies a real action, a real development, something to be understood on the lines of the evolution of *prakṛti* ("nature," or "primordial matter" in Sāṃkhya). On the other hand, Brahman is only "manifested" (*vivartate*) through worldly objects; it merely puts forth an "appearance" (*vivarta*), which is quite difficult to envisage in terms of real creation. In other words, Brahman finds its own "expression" through less-than-real objects and worldly phenomena (a tenet which is more readily associated with the later Advaita Vedānta).

In the second *kārikā*, all of this is restated from a slightly different angle. We come to know that Brahman is the "One" (*ekam eva*), and yet that it is simultaneously presented as an "abode of different powers" (*bhinna-śakti-vyapāśraya*), as their "support" and "resting place." Again, we are dealing with the same problem: if we agree that Brahman is one, that it is essentially "indivisible" (*apṛthaktva*), then it cannot be involved in the process of creation, and the whole of the universe is just an "illusion" (*vivarta*); if, on the other hand, we accept the notion of creation, then Brahman must harbour inherent qualities, distinctions, and "powers." At this point Bhartṛhari tells us that Brahman is both: that "being indivisible, it nevertheless comes to be divided" (*apṛthaktve 'pi . . . pṛthaktveneva vartate*). Curiously enough, the verb used by Bhartṛhari in this passage (*vartate*) essentially implies a real process, a real action—and yet he has chosen this same verb root (in the form of *vivartate*) for Brahman being "manifested" or "appearing" through objects.

In the corresponding prose section of the *Vṛtti* we can find the following passage: "It is maintained that Brahman is essentially beyond any mental constructions (*parikalpa*) and that, having surpassed all differentiations and relations, it is invested with manifold powers (*śakti*); that though it has a form of assuming distinctions between "knowledge" (*vidyā*) and "ignorance" (*avidyā*), it has no distinction at all. And it is not affected either by the beginning or the end in any circumstances, since the latter are brought about by the qualities or the absence of qualities, that are prevalent in empirical practice (*vyavahāra*) and proceed from the repeated experience of different time units (*kāla-bheda*), as well as from the inner force of becoming (*bhāvanā*), associated with different images (*mūrti*).[22] So Brahman is beyond attributes and limitations, including those related to time (something which is readily associated with the process of the real creation of the universe). Indeed, time itself, being closely linked with the concept of causality, with the links of the cause-and-effect chain, becomes vague and elusive—something on a par with "mental constructions" (*parikalpa*). Brahman, it is said, surpasses any distinction or definition (including that of "knowedge" and "ignorance"—the distinction which provided Śaṅkara's Advaita Vedānta with its most powerful ontological cleft between "real" and "unreal"). As Harivṛṣabha tells us somewhat later, this Brahman "seems to divide itself, assuming different and unreal forms. They are similar to the objects that appear in our dreams."[23] Such arguments strongly suggest a *vivarta* theory almost Advaitin in its essence.

However, the same Brahman, as we can recall from Harivṛṣabha's text, is invested "with manifold powers" (*sarvabhiḥ śaktibhir*). It is this Brahman "that produces different modifications (*vikāra*), even those that are merged into the core of the matter—just as in late summer, the turn of the sea-

22. Harivṛṣabha, *Commentary on VP*, 1.1: "Sarvaparikalpātītatattvaṃ bhedasaṃsargasamatikrameṇa samāviṣṭaṃ sarvābhiḥ śaktibhir vidyāvidyāpravibhāgarūpam apravibhāgaṃ kālabheda darśanābhyāsena mūrtivibhāgabhāvanayā ca vyavahārānupātibhir dharmādharmaiḥ sarvāsvavasthāsvanāśritādinidhanaṃ brahmeti pratijñayate /"

23. Harivṛṣabha, *Commentary on VP*, 1.1: ". . . bhedānukāreṇāsatyavibhaktānyarūpopagrāhitā . . . / svapnaviṣayapratibhāsavat /"

son [produces] huge rain clouds."[24] Harivṛṣabha uses one of the most-favoured words in Advaita tradition, namely, "consciousness" (*caitanya*), but he stretches its meaning until it begins to signify something entirely different: "Its consciousness, even though it is one, is split into manifold divisions—just the way the particles of coal [sparks] are present in the flame, or just the way [particles] of water [merge] in the ocean."[25] Actually, the sparks spreading from the flame or the drops of water that are brought together to form the united mass of the ocean present a common enough metaphor for a multitude of "objects" or "beings" that form the universe created by the conscious effort of Saguṇa-Brahman, or Īśvara.

And somewhere in the middle, half-way between those two poles, half-way between those two possibilities of interpretation, Harivṛṣabha is casting about for a solution, a solution hinted at in the *kārikās* of *Vākya-padīya*. Brahman is the "essence of the word" (*śabda-tattva*), or, as the commentator tells us, "[Brahman] is called the essence of the word, since [all of these] modifications (*vikāra*), even though they are believed to have different forms (*bhinna-rūpa*), are derived from [the same] primordial matter (*prakṛti*), because the modifications are involved in words and [vice versa,] the words are involved in modifications."[26] Or, to put it in a different way, the words depend on the objects, when they are trying to express the essence of the universe, but the objects, in turn, depend on the words, which provide inner support and foundation for their very existence; Brahman, being the essence of the word, sustains language in its numerous manifestations (first and foremost, of course, Brahman

---

24. Harivṛṣabha, *Commentary on VP*, 1.1: "prakṛtitvam api prāptān vikārān akaroti saḥ / ṛtudhāmeva grīṣmānte mahato meghasamplavān //"

25. Harivṛṣabha, *Commentary on VP*, 1.1: "tasyaikam api caitanyaṃ bahudhā pravibhajyate / aṅgārāṅkitam utpāte vārirāśer ivodakam //"

26. Harivṛṣabha, *Commentary on VP*, 1.1: "tat tu bhinnarūpābhimatānām api vikārānāṃ prakṛtyanvayitvācchabdopagrāhyatayā śabdopagrāhitayā ca śabdatattvam ity abhidhīyate /"

maintains the inner equilibrium of the Vedas), and the language sustains the whole of the universe. In Harivṛṣabha's commentary there is a reference to some unspecified text which runs as follows: "This subtle speech, which is inseparable in its essence from objects, is one—it is not evolved [outwards]."[27]

Summing up the preceding topics, Harivṛṣabha comes with a preliminary conclusion: "[Mutually] opposing and self-contained powers (*śaktayaḥ*) are reunited in Brahman, which is the essence of the word, without contradicting its unity (*ekatva*)."[28] So, having come full circle, having come back to the concept of Brahman, according to which it is simultaneously presented both as a divided entity and as an indivisible whole, we can only conjecture that the solution of this puzzle might be found in "the essence of the word" (*śabda-tattva*) or "speech" (*vāk*). There should be something in the nature of the word, in the nature of speech or language itself, that accounts for Brahman's curious ability to be both one and many, to be both uniform and infinitely divided.

Of course, this reconciliation of opposite natures comes slightly more easy for Bhartṛhari himself. The very form of the metrical treatise, with its aphoristic formulae and rhetorical declarations, helps to build up the necessary solemn, prophetic mood, which recalls somewhat the mythological pathos of the Upanishads. In the *Vākya-padīya* the "word" is hardly to be regarded as an ordinary, articulated word of everyday speech, it is essentially the divine "speech" (*vāk*) which exists before and beyond the world; it is the speech which creates both the universe and ordinary human language.

In contrast to the Naiyāyikas and the Vaiśeṣikas, who maintained that the main purpose of the language was to supply an appropriate envelope for a non-verbal perception, to organize different perceptions in a quasi-united whole. Bhartṛhari posits the word within the very core of consciousness. While

27. Harivṛṣabha, *Commentary on VP*, 1.1: "sūkṣmām arthenāpravibhaktatattvām ekāṃ vācam anabhiṣyandamānām /"

28. Harivṛṣabha, *Commentary on VP*, 1.2: "ekatvasyāvirodhena śabdatattve brahmaṇi samuccitā virodhinya ātmabhūtāḥ śaktayaḥ /"

the Naiyāyikas and Vaiśeṣikas view words as arbitrary conventions, whose only purpose is to serve as vehicles for their contents, Bhartṛhari's Vedānta right from the start viewed words as playing a much more important role. The Naiyāyikas referred to the example of the infants or deaf-mute people, who are apparently incapable of dealing with words and yet seem to be undoubtedly endowed with consciousness and perfectly able to perceive things; in Bhartṛhari's opinion, at the foundation of every perception or notion we can find its innermost core—a kind of latent, unmanifested word, which forms the "seed" (*bīja*) of thought and consciousness.

This word, which is silently present in the beginning and which is slowly evolving, transforming itself into an actual articulated word—something that can be pronounced and heard, something that is understandable to everybody—can exist in several forms. According to the *Vākya-padīya*, there are three hypostasies, or three aspects of speech: the "seeing" one (*paśyantī*), the "middle" one (*madhyamā*), and the "manifested" one (*vaikharī*).[29] As Bhartṛhari presents it in his treatise,

> This [science of grammar]
> is the supreme and wonderful
> source of knowledge
> for the three-fold speech,
> which combines [in itself] many ways—
> That of the "manifested" [speech],
> that of the "middle" [speech],
> and that of the "seeing" [speech].[30]
> (*Vākya-padīya*, 1.143)

---

29. Strictly speaking, the term *vaikharī* should probably be rendered as "solid," "corporeal" (from *vikhara*, "a solid, dense body"); as we are going to see later, it is certainly related to the plane of solid, tangible objects that constitute the created universe. However, since the degree of reality for this universe still remains undefined, I thought it better to opt for a more neutral word "manifested." Here I was mainly following the suggestion of M. Biardeau, who translated *vaikharī* as "l'étalée [parole]."

30. *VP*, 1.143:

In other words, this speech is prone to reveal itself at first in a latent, "folded-in" state, then in the form of a mental image of the desired object (or else in the grammar paradigms and rules of logical argumentation), and, finally, in the form of an audible usual discourse, in the form of ordinary articulated speech.

For the sake of a more orderly presentation, let us examine a quasi-Neoplatonic scheme suggested by M. Biardeau. The dominant image of her book on Bhartṛhari is the image of Speech (or the Word), which starts its descent from the utmost, totally uniform, and united point, and later goes down, as if dividing itself into a manifold state of empirical diversity. Speech moves away from the initial pure, sinless, unadulterated state of primordial light to the increasingly more "dark," "corrupted," or "obfuscated" states, as if allowing itself to be swamped by the density and opaqueness of inert matter. And, indeed, this Neoplatonic pattern can be partially justified here, since the very mataphor of shining, brilliant, almost dazzling "light" (*prakāśa*) is known to be one of the most favoured Vedāntic images for pure consciousness (*vidyā*, *jñāna*, *caitanya*). Bhartṛhari, in turn, does not hesitate to use the same metaphor for "speech" (*vāk*):

> If consciousness lost
> its eternal similarity
> with the form of speech,[31]
> The light itself would cease to enlighten,
> since it is only this [speech]
> that makes everything recognizable.[32]
> (*Vākya-padīya*, 1.124)

Vaikharyā madhyamāyāś ca paśyantyāś caitad adbhutam /
Anekatīrthabhedāyās trayyā vācaḥ paraṃ padam //

31. "The form of speech" (*vāg-rūpatā*), that is, the "image," "shape," "outline" of speech, but also the "essence" of speech, the "core" of primordial speech, which is ever present as a foundation of the universe.

32. *VP*, 1.124:

It is interesting to note that Harivṛṣabha suggests a tentative explanation for the transformation of this "consciousness-light" into the "form of speech"; he says that if it were not for speech itself, the light would emit its rays forever without anything being clarified (or "seen").[33] In other words, without assuming this form of speech, the light would not even be aware of its own presence.

Vāgrūpatā ced utkrāmed avabodhasya śāśvati /
Na prakāśaḥ prakāśeta sa hi pratyavamarśinī //

33. Harivṛṣabha, *Commentary on VP*, 1.124: "vāgrūpatāyāṃ cāsatyām utpanno 'pi prakāśaḥ pararūpam anaṅgīkurvan prakāśanakriyāsādhanarūpatāyaṃ na vyavatiṣṭhate /"—"If [consciousness] did not assume the form of the word, then, even if the light started to emerge, it would not contribute to the [manifestation] of anything else [besides its own being], and it would be incapable of enlighting [anything else]."

7 Manifestations of Speech

Since it is always easier to understand a subject when we go back to basics or to its simplest forms, let us try to ascertain what it is that corresponds to the level of the "manifested" (*vaikharī*) speech in Bhartṛhari's treatise. This kind of speech exists in some "natural," "material" form before it is split into a multitude of "articulated sounds" (*nāda*).[34] As Harivṛṣabha puts it, "having assumed the form of the syllables (*varṇa*) when the air strikes the points of articulation [as it goes] upwards, manifested speech is related to the breathing activity (*prāṇa-vṛtti*) of those who speak."[35] In Bhartṛhari's words,

---

34. In Abhinavagupta's treatise *Tantra-āloka* ("The Light of Tantra"), "manifested" speech is presented in the following way:

> But the cause of the emergence
> of the phonemes (*varṇa*)
> in their revealed form (*sphuṭa*)
> Is gross manifested [speech] (vaikharī),
> whose effects [become known]
> with the appearance
> of sentences and so on.

> Yā tu sphuṭānāṃ varṇānām utpattau kāraṇaṃ bhavet /
> Sā sthūlā vaikharī yasyāḥ kāryaṃ vākyādi bhūyasā //
> (Abhinavagupta, *Tantra-āloka*, 3.244)

35. Harivṛṣabha, *Commentary on VP*, 1.143: "sthāneṣu vidhṛte vāyau kṛtavarṇaparigrahā / vaikharī vāk prayoktṝṇāṃ prāṇavṛttinibandhanā //."

Having split its uniform essence
into separate forms
of [something] heard,
Having marked in this way separate syllables,
the living breath
is afterwards merged
with those syllables.[36]
(*Vākya-padīya*, 1.115)

In other words, the "living breath" (*prāṇa*), having found its support in the perceptible, "material" air (*vāyu*), comes to be divided into parts or smaller units in accordance with the location and manner of articulation. During this process different phonetic elements take the form of different "syllables" (*varṇa*, lit. "letter"; since in Sanskrit, the alphabet is a syllabary). All these empirical, physically articulated sounds (*nāda*) have their own specific duration, timbre, colouring, and other distinctive features.

It is quite clear that "manifested" (*vaikharī*) speech is essentially a reflection (or expression) of a previous stage, that is, of some preceding activity which takes place on the level of "middle" (*madhyamā*) speech.[37] The "inner," "mental" speech is composed of "ideal sounds" (*dhvani*) or "primordial sounds," sounds in their ideal form. According to Bhartṛhari,

---

36. *VP*, 1.115:

Vibhajan svātmano granthīn śrutirūpaiḥ pṛthagvadaiḥ /
Prāṇo varṇān abhivyajya varṇeṣv evopalīyate //

37. In Kashmir Śaivism the stage of the "middle" (*madhyamā*) speech is characterized primarily by the activity of the speech which, while remaining within the limits of the mental sphere, assumes the duality of the "signified" (*vācya*) and the "signifier" (*vācaka*). It is the speech that has not yet transformed itself into the multitude of articulated sounds and the corresponding multitude of the objects; still, it already has this split, this cleavage within its own nature. As Abhinavagupta says in his *Parātriṃśikā-vivaraṇa* ("The Commentary on the Thirty[-six Ślokas] about the Higher [Goddess]"), "the middle one, in its turn, reveals the duality of the signifier and the signi-

For *sphoṭa*, which is not divided in time,
there is manifested a distinction
in the duration
of ideal sounds (*dhvani*);
And due to the difference
in the conditions [of their] grasping
it is being said
that there is a difference
in the modes
of [their] activity (*vṛtti*).[38]
(*Vākya-padīya*, 1.75)

Let us, for the time being, leave aside that mysterious *sphoṭa*, which appears to be more directly related to the higher Speech, Speech which has not yet entered the process of splitting up. Let us concentrate on the Bhartṛhari's idea of *dhvani* or "ideal sound."

In Patañjali's teaching, *dhvani* is a concrete modus of articulating specific sound (in other words, it directly corresponds to Bhartṛhari's *nāda*). In fact, Patañjali maintained that the very term *sphoṭa* is something that usually refers to a separate phoneme; so, for him *sphoṭa* becomes a name not for the inner "nature," the inner "form" (*svarūpa*) of the word, but rather a term for its specific time of duration (*svakāla*). In other words, it is Patañjali's *sphoṭa* that eventually becomes Bhartṛhari's

---

fied"—"madhyamā punaḥ tayor eva vācyavācakayoḥ bhedam ādarśya . . . /" (Abhinavagupta, *Parātriṃśikā-vivaraṇa* (Srinagar, 1918), 5). In this duality, of course, *vācya* refers both to the objects and to their meanings (another term for this is *artha*), while *vācaka* represents the power that ascribes meanings and contemplates objects. The same duality, which appears on the plane of the "middle" speech is stressed by Bhartṛhari. The corresponding terms in the *Vākya-padīya* are *saṃjñā* for the "signifier," and *saṃjñin* for something "signified," that is, for the object.

38. *VP*, 1.75:

"Sphoṭasyābhinnakālasya dhvanikālānupātinaḥ /
Grahaṇopadhibhedena vṛttibhedaṃ pracakṣate //"

dhvani.[39] Meanwhile, in some of the aesthetical theories, in particular those of Kashmir Śaivism, *dhvani* usually represents an aesthetically interpreted and elaborated "meaning" of a phrase or a poetical "embroidery" (*alaṅkāra*), something to be born inside an indirect, metaphorical use of the words.

For Bhartrhari *dhvani* is, so to speak, an ideal outline, an ideal configuration of a specific syllable, or "phoneme" (*varṇa*). And precisely because of this the "original" or "root" sound has its own distinctive qualities and attributes. In his treatise Bhartṛhari distinguishes between the "original" (*prākṛta*) and the "evolved" (*vaikṛta*) characteristics of the sounds. Among the "original," or "primary" qualities we find a so-called "measure of duration" (*kāla*) which enables us to distinguish phonemes. (According to the rules of Sanskrit phonetics, all sounds are divided into "short" [*hrasva*], "long" [*dīrgha*], and "protracted" [*pluta*] ones.)[40] The "evolved" or "secondary" qualities are related to the external circumstances of pronunciation, and in that they almost coincide with "articulated sounds" or *nāda*.[41]

---

39. In Patañjali's terms, *sphoṭa* is a fundamental sound, while *dhvani* is a concrete, articulated sound, supported by the voice and breath of the speaker ("evaṃ tarhi sphoṭaḥ śabdaḥ / dhvaniḥ śabdaguṇaḥ //"—"And that is why *sphoṭa* is the word itself, while *dhvani* is just an attribute of the word." See Patañjali, *Mahā-bhāṣya* on Pāṇini's *Sūtra*, 1.1.70, and Kātyāyana's *Vārttika*, 5). As K. A. Subramania Iyer puts it, for Patañjali the term *sphoṭa* "is not applied to the meaning-bearing element. There it means only the permanent aspect of a phoneme, shorn of all variations due to special circumstances" (K. A. Subramania Iyer, *Bhartṛhari*, 157). On the differences between Patañjali and Bhartṛhari, see also J. Brough, "Theories of General Linguistics in the Sanskrit Grammarians," in *Transactions of the Philological Society* (Oxford, 1951), 35-37; M. Biardeau, *Théorie de la connaissance*, 256.

40. Strictly speaking, this distinction is valid for the vowels (and it should be borne in mind that "protracted" [*pluta*] vowels can be found only in ancient Vedic texts); consonants are regarded as equal in their duration to a half of a short vowel.

41. In the commentary on the *Vākya-padīya*, it is explained in

In truth, *dhvani* is not something we would normally call a sound; *dhvani* is essentially an ideal, a not-yet-realized sound. When several *dhvanis* are brought together, they reveal a distinctive structure, a primordial construction of a specific word. These root sounds are atomic and indivisible in their nature, they are different from one another, and yet they are regarded as all-pervading (*sarva-gata*) and omnipresent (*vibhu*); they cannot be grasped by the ordinary means of perception. They act as an "efficient cause" (*nimitta*), as a necessary preliminary premise for the emitting of the actual, empirical sound. Most importantly, we are capable of mentally pronouncing them even before they are articulated, we are capable of mentally recognizing them when someone is speaking: we can still distinguish different sounds whatever the faults or peculiarities of the concrete way of pronouncing them. Somewhat later we are going to come back to the specific mechanism of this "recognition" (*pratyabhijñā*).

Finally, the higher stage in the three-fold division of speech suggested by Bhartṛhari corresponds to the stage of the "seeing" (*paśyantī*) speech.[42] Harivṛṣabha's elaborates on this theme in his commentary: "But the higher form of the seeing speech does not embrace erroneous forms, it is unrelated and rests beyond worldly practice (*loka-vyavahāra*). And it is precisely about this speech that it is said in some [parts] of the

---

the following words: "Original sound is considered to be the cause of the word perception, while the evolved sound is the preliminary premise of the differences in the specific position [during pronunciation]"—"śabdasya grahaṇe hetuḥ prākṛto dhvanir iṣyate / sthitibhede nimittatvaṃ vaikṛtaḥ pratipadyate //" (Harivṛṣabha, *Commentary on the "Vākya-padīya,"* 1.76). Actually, Harivṛṣabha cites this passage, referring the reader to the *Saṃgraha* ("The Collection") of the grammarian Vyāḍi.

42. In Kashmir Śaivism the "seeing" speech, though staying beyong the duality of the "signifier" (*vācaka*) and the "signified" (*vācya*), is already pregnant with the inner "power of desire" (*icchā-śakti*). As Somānanda puts it in his *Śiva-dṛṣṭi* ("The Seeing of Śiva"),

sacred tradition: it can be approached either through grammar, which supplies knowledge of the correctness [of word forms], or through [special] yoga, which is primarily [concerned] about the word."[43] Somewhat earlier, in the commentary on the same *kārikā*, Harivṛṣabha notes in a quite significant passage:

> The "seeing" [speech] is wholly permeated with the power of successive [evolution], which gives the order of successive [steps], even though it [still] remains undifferentiated. Whether moving or immovable, whether grasped by mental concentration, hidden or pure, whether having in itself the form of the objects of consciousness, whether having shed that form or being devoid of form altogether, whether assuming the appearence of separate [external] objects, whether assuming the appearance of connected [internal] objects or the appearance of the absence of all objects, this ["seeing" speech] has [potential] differences without any [actual] evolution.[44]

Most of the traits attributed to the "seeing" speech, are set in groups of three—which might be regarded as an indirect indi-

---

The seeing [speech]
is indeed the acting . . . /

Paśyantī hi kriyā . . . /
(Somānanda, *Śiva-dṛṣṭi*, 2.83)

However, this action exists only in its latent form, as a kind of a potency which is about to be realized.

43. Harivṛṣabha, *Commentary on VP*, 1.143: "paraṃ tu paśyantīrūpam anapabhraṃśaṃ asaṅkīrṇaṃ lokavyavahārātītam / tasyā eva vāco vyākaraṇena sādhutvajñānalabhyena vā śabdapūrveṇa yogenādhigamyata ity ekeṣām āgamaḥ /

44. Harivṛṣabha, *Commentary on VP*, 1.143: "pratisaṃhṛtakramā satyapyabhede samāviṣṭakramaśaktiḥ paśyantī / sā calācala pratilabdhasamādhānā cāvṛtā viśuddhā ca sanniviṣṭajñeyākārā pratilīnākārā nirākārā ca paricchinnārthapratyavabhāsā saṃsṛṣṭārthapratyavabhāsā praśāntasarvārthapratyavabhāsā cety aparimāṇabhedā /" This passage on the "seeing" speech is almost literally cited in

cation that for Bhartṛhari and Harivṛṣabha the first three stages of speech are completely integrated within the third one.

Despite some vacillations in terminology that beset the author of the treatise at this point, the higher stage is usually represented by *sphoṭa*, or uniform, indivisible Speech, which ultimately is concentrated in one sound. Without going into further details, we can note that *sphoṭa* is present in every word of the spoken language, where it reveals the word's own "inner form" (*svarūpa*). Being one (and right now we are leaving aside the problem, whether it is the one and the same for all the words, one for each single phrase, or, indeed, one for every single word taken separately), *sphoṭa* is grasped suddenly, immediately, in a single act—without any intermediary stages in the process of perception. Or, to put it in Bhartṛhari's words,

> And in the same way,
> owing to previous perceptions
> [that are left] unnamed
> but contribute to the ultimate
> clear perception,

Abhinavagupta's *Īśvara-pratyabhijñā-vivṛtti-vimarśinī* ("The [Treatise] on the Subtle Intuition, Leading to the Recognition of the Lord"): "tad āha tatrabhavān bhartṛhariḥ pratisaṃhṛtakram--ntaḥ saty apy abhede samāviṣṭa kramaśaktiḥ paśyantī / Sā acalā ca calā pratilabdhasamādhānā ca sanniviṣṭajñeyākārā pratilīnākārā nirākārā ca paricchinnārthapratyavabhāsā praśāntapratyavabhāsā ca /"—"And thus the venerable Bhartṛhari said: "The 'seeing' [speech] is regarded as the power of successive [evolution], which gives the order of successive [steps], even though it [still] remains undifferentiated. It is moving and immovable, and it is grasped by mental concentration; it can take the form of the objects of perception, or it can shed this form, or it can be devoid of form altogether; it can assume the appearance of separate [external] objects, or it can assume the appearance of [their] absence" (Abhinavagupta, *Īśvara-pratyabhijñā-vivṛtti-vimarśinī*, Kashmir Series of Texts and Studies, LXII, 1941, vol. II, 226); incidentally, M. Biardeau presents a later passage as being allegedly cited by Abhinavagupta. As we can see, Abhinavagupta attributes this passage to Bhartṛhari himself.

The inner form of the word
is suddenly revealed
when it is illumined [from inside]
by the ideal sound.[45]
(*Vākya-padīya*, 1.83)

In other words, the specific, distinctive trait of the third stage of Speech is the way it is grasped. It might seem to a respective addressee that he is grasping the meaning of an utterance gradually, in successive steps. He might even think that the meaning is slowly evolving while the sentence is being pronounced. Actually, the sense of the phrase can only flash out suddenly; it can only be revealed as a uniform whole; and it can only shine forth after the phrase is completed and its meaning recognized.

---

45. VP, 1.83:

Pratyayair anupākhyeyair grahaṇānuguṇais tathā /
Dhvaniprakāśite śabde svarūpam avadhāryate //

8 Language and Being

The teaching of Bhartṛhari cannot be summed up by the concept of an indissoluble relation between cognition and language. He takes another step forward in order to link language and being, in order to investigate the ontological foundations of such a connection. And here the necessary link is supplied by the identification of the perceived object (*grāhya*), of the perceiving subject (*grāhaka*), as well as the state of perception itself (*grahaṇa*). All of them merge in the "fourth" state of speech. The fourth stage is the stage which appears in Harivṛṣabha's commentary on one of the above-mentioned *kārikās*, but it also came to be mentioned indirectly in the treatise of Bhartṛhari.[46] The fourth state of speech is called the "higher" one (or *parā vāk*). In the words of Harivṛṣabha's commentary,

---

46. The assumption of the existence of a fourth state of speech became one of the most important theoretical tenets of the 'Pratyabhijñā' school of Kashmir Śaivism. Abhinavagupta, for whom the higher stage (known as *parā vāk*—"the higher speech") was a corner-stone of the whole system, criticizes Bhartṛhari precisely because the higher speech is not directly mentioned in the *Vākya-padīya*. But, of course, *parā vāk* was very prominent in Harivṛṣabha's commentary. (For some unknown reason André Padoux seems to overlook this, saying that the notion of the "higher speech is totally absent both from the *Vākya-padīya* and from its *Vṛtti*). In his *Parātriṃśikā-vivaraṇa* Abhinavagupta presents *parā vāk* as the real foundation of all other forms of speech, as well as of all the existing universe: "This higher [state] is really present on the level of the "seeing" [speech], as well as on all the others. If it were not on the

> this three-fold speech, which is similar to the illusory appearence of the "knots" of consciousness, whose dimensions cannot be determined, is shining within [all] human beings because of the fourth [state]. And here, too, only a part of this [speech] is used in ordinary practice (*vyavahāra*), while the rest stays beyond practice common [to all]. It was said: "Speech is measured by four quarters, and it is known to the wise ones among brahmans. Three of these [quarters] are immovable, being hidden in a secret place; human beings speak only with the fourth [quarter] of speech."[47] The pure form of speech is totally supported by the traditional knowledge . . . which is called grammar.[48]

This ultimate unity of the speech is revealed in the sacred, initial word of the Vedas, though the sacred texts here are taken in their "purified" form, that is, in a form free of human error. It is the core of this "folded-in," but still invisibly existing word that serves as an initial matrix and is used at the beginning of each successive world cycle for the creation of the universe. As it is said in the *Vākya-padīya*,

> The knowers of the sacred tradition
> know that this [world]

---

level of the "seeing" [speech], as well as on all the others, darkness would result and unconsciousness would follow"—"tad uttaraṃ paśyantyādidaśasv api vastuto vyavasthitā tayā vinā paśyantyādiṣu aprakāśatapattyā jaḍaṭāprasaṅgāt" (*Parātriṃśikā-vivaraṇa*, p. 5).

47. This passage is taken from *Ṛg-Veda*, 1.164.45. Note that the sequence of the stages here is reversed.

48. Harivṛṣabha, *Commentary on VP*, 143: "saiṣā trayī vāk caitanyagranthivivartavad anākhyeyaparimāṇā turīyeṇa manuṣyeṣu pratyavabhāsate / tatrāpi cāsyāḥ kiṃ cid eva vyāvahārikam anyat tu sāmānyavyavahārātītam / āha ca catvāri vāk parimitā padāni tāni vidur brāhmaṇā ye manīṣiṇaḥ / guhā trīṇi nihitā neṅgayanti turīyaṃ vāco manuṣyā vadanti // iti // tasyāś cāsaṅkīrṇaṃ vāco rūpaṃ kārtsnyena . . . vyākaraṇākhye nibaddham /"

is just an evolution of the word,
And that all of this [universe][49]
is first manifested
owing to the Vedic verse.[50]
(*Vākya-padīya*, 1.120)

The sacred word, which is posited at the very source of the world as an indivisible unity and yet as a creative matrix producing all existing things, is also the higher Brahman of the Upanishadic texts, symbolized by the sacred mantra *Oṃ* (usually referred to as *praṇava*). Strictly speaking, the syllable *Oṃ*, which is presented in the form of a "protracted," resounding mantra (*praṇava* literally means something "resounding," "throbbing," "echoing in resonance") has two functions. On the one hand, it links Brahman and any specific, concrete Vedic text, since it is this mantra from which the Vedas are eventually created anew in the beginning of each successive world cycle. On the other hand, it is a link between Brahman and the multitude of existing things re-created in each successive universe. In other words, the sacred syllable *Oṃ* helps to create both the objects of perception and knowledge and is the means leading to this knowledge.

In Bhartṛhari's words,

The true knowledge,
which is called the pure one,
is attained through the one and only word.

---

49. "All of this [universe]" (*etad viśvam*); that is, all of this created world, whic is perceived as full of living souls and inanimate objects, *viśva* being the first state of the "cosmic" manifestation of Brahman. In Gauḍapāda's *Kārikās*, *viśva* corresponds to the first "step" of consciousness, to that of its "waking" (*jāgarita*) stage. Here it corresponds to the first stage of speech which is evolving or manifesting itself in the world.

50. VP, 1.120:

Śabdasya pariṇāmo 'yam ity āmnāyavido viduḥ /
Chandobya eva prathamam etad viśvaṃ vyavartate //

It is bound
by the form of the [syllable] *Oṃ* . . .[51]
(*Vākya-padīya*, 1.9)

At first glance, this appears to be a coherent system of ideas. At the apex of the pyramid we find "pure knowledge" (*viśuddhis . . . vidyā*), which probably corresponds to Śaṅkara's concept of "pure ātman" (or "pure" Brahman devoid of any qualities, *nirguṇa-brahma*). Meanwhile, the sacred mantra *Oṃ* represents the "face" of the *saguṇa-brahma* or "lower" Brahman, Brahman the Creator (*īśvara*)—the face which is benignly turned towards us at the beginning of each universe cycle. Indeed, one must admit that Bhartṛhari supplies us with ample evidence in favour of this interpretation; he keeps saying in his treatise that the syllable *Oṃ* gives us the true "image" (*anukāra*) of Brahman, while at the same time presenting the true "image" of all sacred Vedic texts (*sarva-śruti-rūpa*). Finally, in the second part of the third chapter of *Vākya-padīya*, where Bhartṛhari discusses the notion of the "substance" (*dravya*), we find a more elaborate definition of the "pure knowledge" or "pure consciousness" (*śuddha jñāna*):

Owing to [the existence]
of many forms everywhere,
"purity" [is posited] for consciousness,
which is devoid of any support;
That is why the highest purity,
which is one,
is said to be devoid of form.[52]
(*Vākya-padīya*, 3.2.56)

---

51. VP, 1.9:

Satyā viśuddhis tatroktā vidyaivaikapadāgamā /
Yuktā praṇavarūpeṇa . . . //

52. VP, 3.2.56:

Sarvatha rūpatā śuddhiḥ jñānasya nirupāśrayā /
Tato 'py asya parāṃ śuddhim eke prāhur arūpikām //

And this is where the difficulties start. In Advaita Vedānta, "pure consciousness" is certainly regarded as devoid of "forms," since it is essentially devoid of any qualities or attributes. In Bhartṛhari's Vedānta, "pure consciousness" is postulated only theoretically; in reality that highest point, the higher Brahman itself contains within its own being a multitude of potential forms, a multitude of manifestations that until the very moment of creation remain in a peculiar involved, latent state.

As mentioned above, Brahman in Bhartṛhari's treatise is identified with the Word (*śabda*) or with Speech (*vāk*). The *kārikās* of the *Vākya-padīya* do not yet use the term *śabda-brahma* ("Brahman-Word"); it makes its first appearance only in Harivṛṣabha's Commentary. In any event, here Bhartṛhari deviates slightly from the tradition of the Upanishads. For instance, in the *Maitri Upanishad* we find the matter clearly stated:

> Come to know of the two Brahmans—
> Brahman-Word and the higher [Brahman].
> Having left behind Brahman-Word,
> one should go to the higher Brahman.[53]
> (*Maitri Upanishad*, 6.22)

It is clear that in the Upanishadic verse "Brahman-Word" (*śabda-brahma*) signifies Brahman as an object of ritual worship. In Śaṅkara's system it would correspond to the level of *saguṇa-brahma* (that of the Brahman with [many auspicious] qualities) or *īśvara* (personified God, God the Creator, the omniscient, omnipresent and merciful Lord). From the standpoint of Advaita Vedānta, of course, this concept of *śabda-brahma* represents a lower, limited, even illusory stage in the knowledge of Brahman.[54] As it is explained subsequently in the *Maitri*

---

53. *Maitryupaniṣad*, 6.22:

Dve brahmaṇi veditavye śabdabrahma paraṃ ca yat /
Śabdabrahmaṇi niṣṇataḥ paraṃ brahmādhigacchati //

54. It is something that in Śaṅkara's system came to be branded

Upanishad, in the prose gloss on the above-cited verse, "one should meditate on two Brahmans: on the Word, as well as on something other than the Word. It is only through the Word that something other than the Word is revealed. And the [syllable] *Oṃ* is the Word. Through the [syllable] *Oṃ* the Word goes upwards and merges into something other than the Word."[55]

This conception of the Word or *Oṃ* recalls Gauḍapāda's *Māṇḍūkya-kārikā*:

> Indeed, the syllable *Oṃ*
> is the lower Brahman,
> and the same syllable *Oṃ*
> is held to be the higher Brahman.[56]
> (*Māṇḍūkya-kārikā*, 1.26)

It certainly looks as if we've encountered here a somewhat different branch of the Upanishadic tradition. Remember, too, the famous verse of the *Praśna Upanishad* (5.2): "O Satyakāma, the very same Brahman [which is known] both as the higher and as the lower one, is the syllable *Oṃ*."[57] Again, note that the higher and the lower hypostases of Brahman are

---

with the term *vyāvahārika-jñāna*, that is, "empirical," "conventional," "pragmatically convenient" knowledge. In Advaita Vedānta this "empirical knowledge," or "empirical consciousness," stands in absolute opposition to the concept of "the higher knowledge" or "knowledge from the standpoint of the higher truth" (*pāramārthika-jñāna*), which is ultimately identified with the higher Brahman. So, "empirical knowledge" is nothing but a convenient tool in the workaday world, while "the higher knowledge" can never become instrumental and ultimately coincides with its own goal—that is, the *nirguṇa-brahma* ("Brahman devoid of attributes"), or the "pure *ātman*."

55. *Maitryupaniṣad*, 6.22: "dve brahmaṇi abhidhyeye śabdaś cāśabdaś cātha śabdenaivāśabdam aviṣkriyate 'tha tatra oṃ iti śabdo 'nenordhvam utkranto 'śabde nidhānam iti . . . /"

56. Gauḍapāda, *Māṇḍūkya-kārikā*, 1.26:

Praṇavo hy aparaṃ brahma praṇavaś ca paraḥ smṛtaḥ /

57. *Praśnopaniṣad*, 5.2: "etad vai satyakāma paraṃ cāparaṃ

ultimately brought together through the power of that primordial sacred mantra.

So, Vedānta theoretically allows us to regard Brahman not only as pure consciousness—which sometimes comes to reflect fleeting, accidental, or even totally illusory phenomena—but also as a specific entity, full of its own inner activity, full of potencies or "seeds" (*bīja*) of becoming. That is how Bhartṛhari words it in his treatise:

> This willing desire, called the word,
> has a nature similar to that
> of an egg;
> Its evolving starts gradually,
> when one part follows another,
> just as it happens
> when [one foot follows another
> during ordinary] walking.[58]
> (*Vākya-padīya*, 1.51)

Commenting on this *kārikā*, Harivṛṣabha explains that the egg mentioned here is actually a peacock's egg (*mayūra-āṇḍa*).[59] And it is a singularly appropriate example since the yellow

---

ca brahma yad oṃkāraḥ /"

58. VP, 1.51:

Āṇḍabhāvam ivāpanno yaḥ kratuḥ śabdasaṃjñakaḥ /
Vṛttis tasya kriyārūpā bhāgaśo labhate kramam //

59. Harivṛṣabha, *Commentary on VP*, 1.51: "Having ceased to assume all its distinctions, the outward word of the ordinary practice disappears inside the 'internal organ,' as if inside the [uniform] colour of the peacock's egg-yolk, but it still does not lose previously acquired distinctions, [that stay inside] in the original form of potentialities"—"sarvavibhāgodgrāhapratisaṃhāreṇa bāhyo vyāvahārikaḥ śabdo 'ntaḥkaraṇe mayūrādyāṇḍarasavat pūrvavibhāgodgrāhabhāvanāmātrām avyatikrāman pratilīyate /" The "internal organ" (*antaḥ-karaṇa*), mentioned in Harivṛṣabha's text, is composed of *buddhi* ("intellectual will," "reason," the ability to make intellectually sound decisions), *manas* ("mind," or the integrator of all sense per-

egg-yolk, which at first glance seems to be entirely uniform, is already harboring inside all the multicolored splendor of the mature bird's feathers. This simile of the peacock's egg-yolk became a favourite metaphor for the potencies of Brahman in Kashmir Śaivism.[60] In any case, pure Brahman, which appears to be perfectly uniform and always equal to its own being, seems to be concealing different "powers," "potencies," "potentialities" (*śakti*, *bhavanā*) within this seeming self-eqation. It is enough to remember the above-cited *kārikā*:

> It is [taught] by the sacred tradition
> to be one and the only—
> yet it is the abode of different powers;
> And so, being indivisible,

---

ceptions), and *ahaṃkara* ("ego," "individual personality"). What is implied here is the reverse movement of the "word" or "speech," when it gradually withdraws its tentacles from the outward "waking" perceptions in order to start moving towards its own inner nature. The first step is, of course, its merging into the "internal" (in Bhartṛhari's terms, "middle"—*madhyamā*) state, when it is essentially manifested as a purely mental activity. And all the "potencies" (*bhavanā*) that inherently stay with the speech on its way back, are the same potencies that originally surged from inside, stimulating Speech to start the creation of the Universe.

60. Another allegory, popular with the Kashmir Śaivite writers and conveying the same image of a thrusting forward, bursting forth potency, is that of the seed of a banyan tree. See, for instance, *Parātriṃśikā-kārikā*, 24:

> Just as a great banyan tree
> is present in its seed
> only in the form of potency,
> So the whole of the universe,
> with its moving and immovable things,
> is present in the heart
> [of the higher Lord].

Yathā nyagrodhabījasthaḥ śaktirūpo mahādrumaḥ /
Tathā hṛdayabījasthaṃ viśvam etac carācaram //

it nevertheless comes to be divided
owing to these powers.[61]
(*Vākya-padīya*, 1.2)

These potentialities evolve to become the world, but, according to the previous *kārikā* (1.51), this is not a linear evolution taking place in time. Bhartṛhari, when he speaks of the successive movements of the legs being repeated in ordinary walking, is referring to the alternating expansion and contraction of the world cycles. It cannot be regarded as a gradual emanation, since it is presented rather as a dialectical swing which oscillates back and forth, as a pulsating wave of tension that rises and falls.

The very term "Brahman" (*brahma*) is derived from a verb root *bṛh*, which means "to spread," "to grow," "to swell," "to expand." However, in order to indicate Brahman's ability to evolve into the world, Bhartṛhari makes prominent use of another word found in *Māṇḍūkya-kārikā*: the famous term *spanda*, meaning "vibration," "pulsation," "throbbing," or even "shimmering." Moreover, in his treatise on grammar he keeps referring to a "flashing up," "flaring up," "exploding from within." (One could cite numerous derivations from the root *sphuṭ*, including the truly remarkable *sphoṭa*, as well as derivations from a similar—both phonetically and contextually—verb root, *sphur*). Also, one should consider that the root *sphuṭ* has yet another shade of meaning: it conveys the idea of something "suddenly manifested," "suddenly apparent, evident." And the use of *sphoṭa* here signifies not only the "manifestation," "appearance," or the "revelation of sense," but also a specific state of consciousness when, in response to the pronounced word, our mind is suddenly illuminated with the corresponding image. The "flashing up" of the mental image, which is triggered by the word, is astonishingly close to a certain concept of the creation where the whole universe is sud-

61. VP, 1.2:

Ekam eva yad āmnātam bhinnaśaktivyapāśrayat /
Apṛthaktve 'pi śaktibhyaḥ pṛthaktvena ca vartate //

denly manifested the moment it is called by its true and proper name. A sound wave, then, may be the most appropriate analogy to convey the idea of this "flashing up" or "pulsation" of something coming into existence. For it conjures up the image not only of a pulsating light but also the reverberating echo of an intoned mantra. And while we are prepared to concede that the four Vedas do provide us with a true enough "image" (*anukāra*, *rūpa*) of Brahman, we should remember that this "picture" or "image" is primarily a sonoric one.

Actually, we are now approaching, from a slightly different angle, the very problem that became so interesting in respect to Gauḍapāda's treatise. The same question arises: Are we dealing with the real creation of the world—or is it a mere "manifestation" of some entity which is essentially eternal and immovable? Is there a place for a real evolution of the universe—or is it the meaning, which for some reason remained hidden, that becomes suddenly revealed (*prakāśate*) both in words and in their corresponding objects? Is there, in general, any difference between "creation" and "expression," between the evolution of the world and the "illumination" of the meaning—or are they essentially identical, since every object and every being (*bhāva*) in this universe is nothing but a manifestation of the same Word, a mere variation in the aesthetical shades of meaning that can be ascribed to one and the same primordial syllable?

After all, the verb most favored by Bhartṛhari in this context is *vṛt*, with all its derivations and connotations, including "appearance" and "seeming illusion" (*vivarta*). As the author tries to explain in the very beginning of his treatise,

> And in different schools it is clear
> that the [expressive] power of the words
> remains the same.[62]
>
> (*Vākya-padīya*, 1.6)

---

62. VP, 1.6:

Śabdānāṃ yataśaktitvaṃ tasya śākhāsu dṛśyate //

This means that the expressive power of words cannot be separated from their "activity" or "efficacity"; "expression" means "effecting" something; it is capable of producing effects, hence it is capable of creation. In Bhartṛhari's text, every time we come across the mention of certain "powers" or "potencies" (*śakti*) that are regarded as indispensable to Brahman and inseparable from it, we should bear in mind that one of the most important "powers" implied in this set is an "expressive power" (*abhidhā-śakti*) or "means of expression" used in a poetical text. And, as Harivṛṣabha aptly puts it in his commentary on this *kārikā*, "the [expressive] power of the words remains the same, since they are capable of corresponding to this particular object, as well as of producing this particular pleasure (*abhyudaya*)."[63] What Harivṛṣabha means here is not merely an aesthetic pleasure derived from a masterful use of words, but the much more important concept of bliss and its direct bearing upon the possibility of liberation.[64] This "power of words" is prominent both in the creative urge manifested on the cosmological plane of existence and in its aesthetic counterpart found in the creative activity of a poet. Similarly, we can recognize in all the varying interpretations of the Veda,[65] the same uniform creative power, the same uniform Brahman.

---

63. Harivṛṣabha, *Commentary on VP*, 1.6: "śabdānāṃ yataśaktitvam / tathārthapratyāyane sāmarthyāt tathābhyudayahetutvāt /" Or, in this respect we might be reminded of Kātyāyana's commentary on Pāṇini: "If, having started with the study of *śāstras*, one [learns] to use [language properly], one attains the same bliss as in using Vedic words"—"śāstrapūrvake prayoge 'bhyudayas tat tūlyaṃ vedaśabdena /" (Kātyāyana, *Vārttika*, 1.10.21).

64. Incidentally, that is why K. A. Subramania Iyer in his English translation of Harivṛṣabha's commentary renders *abhyudaya* as "merit"—obviously trying to emphasize its religious connotations. While I happen to disagree with him on this point, I can still appreciate the idea behind his interpretation. See K. A. Subramania Iyer, *The Vākyapadīya of Bhartṛhatri with the Vṛtti*, English translation (Poona: Deccan College, 1965), 9.

65. In Bhartṛhari's words,

Finally, there is yet another "power" (*śakti*) of Brahman introduced by Bhartṛhari. It is the power of *vikalpa* ("imagination," "fantasy," "mental constructions"). In the opinion of M. Biardeau, the teachings of Bhartṛhari clearly introduce the concept of two different planes, or two different vectors of evolution and differentiation: the first is represented by the empirical multifold intertwining of universal powers (they can be described as "powers" or *śaktayaḥ* par excellence), while the second embraces the corresponding variations of mental constructions or "imaginary inventions" (*kalpanā*). According to the French scholar, both of these planes of existence should be regarded as mutually correlating, as being subjected to some pre-established "harmony" or coordination, though, at the same time, they never overlap one another and should never be considered as identical. Viewed from this standpoint, the very notion of *śakti* begins to resemble a peculiar magical power which eventually organizes the universe into a coherent whole and transforms it into an orderly cosmos. In Biardeau's words, "The absolute is patterned—if it is possible to say this—according to the model of some formula which is pronounced in order to obtain the desired result. But to believe in magic means to believe in the reality of its effects."[66]

I do not find this postulate of an opposition between the power which is engaged in creating the universe and the power

---

Both the means of knowing
    and the sign (*anukāra*)
    of this [one] is the Veda;
Even though it is one,
    it is interpreted by the sages
    in many ways.

(*Vākya-padīya*, 1.5)

Prāptyupāyo 'nukaraś ca tasya vedo mahārṣibhiḥ /
Eko 'py anekavartmeva samāmnātaḥ pṛthak pṛthak //

66. "l'Absolu est modelé—si l'on ose dire—sur le type d'une formule, que l'on prononce pour obtenir tel resultat desiré. Mais croire à magie signifie précisément que l'on croit à la realité de ses effects."—M. Biardeau, *Théorie de la connaissance*, 282.

of "imagination" or "expression" entirely convincing. It is too forced and hardly justified. Indeed, in the third chapter of the *Vākya-padīya*, in the part dealing with the idea of space (*dik*), Bhartṛhari comes back to the term *kalpanā*. It is discussed in the following way:

> The imaginary division
> of time and space
> is established in the world
> in accordance [with a similar division]
> in [our] consciousness.
> And who would have wished for another
> natural [state]
> for living beings?[67]
> (*Vākya-padīya*, 3.6.18)

Of course, Biardeau's argument is to some extent justified since she is attempting to show us how Bhartṛhari adapted and transformed certain Buddhist concepts in order to make them more "real" or "ontologized." However, I believe that the recurrence of such roots as *vikḷp* ("to invent," "to imagine"), *vivṛt*, and *vṛt* ("to manifest," "to make evident," or "to be manifested," "to appear") actually brings us back to the image of the universe suggested by Gauḍapāda.

"Creation" here is simultaneously regarded as "expression," or even as a "manifestation" of the hidden meaning, since the actual, cosmological aspect of the universe is no more "real" than its mental aspect. Brahman, which is manifested as Speech, is essentially neither a tangle of natural phenomena, nor a mere combination of words or their meanings. The Brahman-Word (*śabda-brahma*) is nothing but a perpetual shimmering, perpetual pulsation of meanings, images, things. Elements themselves are interchangeable, they dissolve and melt away, they disappear only to be replaced by new ones;

67. VP, 3.6.18:

Caitanyavat sthitā loke dikkālaparikalpanā /
Prakṛtiṃ prāṇīnāṃ taṃ hi ko 'nyatha sthapayiṣyati //

what remains immovable is the energetical charge, which again and again brings along the same structure, the same set of elements, the same pattern of being.

It is by no means accidental that in Bhartṛhari's treatise we encounter the same familiar image of a shimmering, glowing fire-brand. The torch, which has almost burnt down, still whirls in a circle, and it goes fast enough for us to be aware not of its respective positions, respective points in space, but only of the glowing circle, of the pulsating motion itself. As Bhartṛhari puts it,

> Whether [everything is presented]
> as [coming from]
> the [inner] Self (*svamātra*),
> or as [coming from]
> the higher [Brahman] (*paramātra*)—
> it is still defined by the word;
> Since it is only owing to the word
> that the meaning[68] is established.
> And even in entirely different circumstances,
> [when there is no substrate,
> and the only entity present]
> is the efficient cause,
> For example, when we get
> a circle of fire (*alāta-cakra*)
> [outlined by the burning fire-brand,]
> owing to the mere power of the word
> its form becomes clearly revealed
> [in our mind].[69]
>
> (*Vākya-padīya*, 1.129-30)

---

68. "Meaning" (*artha*). For that matter, it is even possible to say in this case that "only owing to the word the object itself is established," since *artha* might signify both the "meaning" ("something connoted") and the "object" of consciousness ("something denoted").

69. VP, 1.129-30):

Svamātrā paramātrā vā śrutyā prakramyate yathā /
Tathaiva rūḍhatāmeti tayā hy artho vidhīyate //

And it is no coincidence, either, that the "knowledge" of Brahman (and ultimately this knowledge is equal to the "attainment" of Brahman) coincides with the realization of the meaning of the primordial Word—the realization, which becomes possible only in an act of a sudden illumination, or (to put it in Western terms) an act of "intellectual intuition" (*pratibhā*). Instead of trying to decide what should be regarded as relatively more "real," whether it is "pure Brahman" or Brahman endowed with latent "powers," instead of being forced to chose between the reality of cosmological creation and the more evasive reality of "expression," we can take a different track that brings us straight to the concept of "pulsation," a "shimmering" or oscillating wave of meaning, a "pattern" or "net" which is totally devoid of any substrate.

Atyantam atathābhūte nimitte śrutyupāśrayāt /
Dṛśyate 'lātacakrādau vastvākāranirūpaṇā //

Incidentally, the two states tentatively defined here as "inner Self" (*svamātra*, lit., "solely Oneself") and "higher Brahman" (*paramātra*, that is, "solely Another" or "solely the Higher one"), roughly correspond to the two higher states in Gauḍapāda's table: to that of the "deep sleep" (*suṣupti*, *supta*) and to that of the ineffable *turīya* ("the fourth one"). In his commentary Harivṛṣabha presents them as two distinct views held, respectively, by the believers in "inner consciousness" (*caitanya*) ("consciousness, the womb of all beings, spreads out like oil squeezed from sesame seeds"—"caitanyaṃ bhūtayonis tilakṣodarasavat pravibhajyata . . . /"), and by the believers in the transcendent eternal Brahman ("just like sparks [coming] from the great fire, like a mass of clouds [gathered] by light wind, like sprinkles of water [streaming] from a broken moon-stone, or just like *sala* trees [growing] out of the soil, or else like banyan trees [pushing] their air-roots down from the banyan seeds . . ."—"tad yathā mahato 'gner vispuliṅgaḥ sūkṣmād vāyor abhraghanāścandrakāntād vibhāginyas toyadhārāḥ pṛthivyā vā sālādayo nyagrodhadhānābhyo vā sāvarohaprasavā nyagrodhā . . . /")—Harivṛṣabha, *Commentary on the VP*, 1.129. However, it is not difficult to see that in both Bhartṛhari's and Gauḍapāda's teachings these two approaches to the creation of the world and its objects, far from contradicting each other, are actually complementary.

Language reality, or—to use the words of Bhartṛhari and Harivṛṣabha—pure "Speech" (*vāk*) is neither a fixed and stable substance (though it is still regarded as the very core of the universe), nor is it an envelope, an outer shell, a means of transmitting some deeper sense. Language "thinks itself," or, more precisely, it "utters itself," it is again and again engaged in its own interplay, in sending itself forth as an energy wave, as a "vibration," as a perpetual throb which reproduces itself in a fixed, self-organizing pattern. And the pattern itself is ever devoid of any substrate or foundation—it exists without ever being materialized.[70]

This creative activity, which takes place on the universal, cosmic scale, is being replayed and re-created again on the level of separate mental structures of the "speaker" and the "listener." Or, more precisely, it is not even replayed or reflected, since the process of "speaking forth" remains one and the same, so that the whole of the worldly evolution is

---

70. Note that the notion of *pratibhā*, or sudden insight, sudden "flashing up" of the true knowledge, which plays such an important part in Abhinavagupta's version of Śaivism, is also regarded as a specific state "between" two entities, as a vibrating and live interjunction between two fixed points. *Pratibhā* gives an adept a direct insight into the primordial self-awareness, the primordial consciousness. Nevertheless, it is essentially an intermediating pulsation, an oscillation and interplay between two elements. In the words of Abhinavagupta, "this consciousness, which is praised by the Āgama texts as an "insight" (*pratibhā*), as an "evolving" (*unmeṣa*) and so on, stays in the interval between two dual cognitions, when the first one is already finished, and the second one has not yet appeared"—"bhavati cedam astamitodeṣyadubhayakalpajñānāntaralāvartyunmeṣapratibhādiśabdāgamagītam . . . /" (Abhinavagupta, *Parātriṃśikāvivaraṇa*, p. 106). Everything here seems to depend on the ability of the adept to retain this ambivalent and tense oscillation, everything is focused upon the art of staying between two points of reference. For Abhinavagupta this self-awareness is still regarded primarily as a psychological or cosmological reality; what matters for Bhartṛhari is the energy pattern which is clearly discerned in the sudden "illumination" of *pratibhā*.

being reiterated anew in every meaningful utterance. We can assume that every act of speech is similar to a sudden flash of light, which again and again—like an enlarger lamp in a photographer's dark room—develops the same latent pattern and makes it visible to us. Bhartṛhari puts it in the following way:

> When the mental idea (*buddhi*),
> whose seeds (*bīja*) were sown
> by the articulated sounds (*nāda*),
> is finally fully grown
> with its last [evoked] sound (*dhvani*),
> The whole of the word
> is suddenly determined.[71]
> (*Vākya-padīya*, 1.84)

Again, what we encounter here is the "vibration" of the primordial Word. At first it dwells in the mind of the speaker in an involved state, as a mere "seed" (*bīja*) of preconceived meaning, then it is "materialized" as if "embodied" in the articulated sounds of ordinary speech. As soon as a word is pronounced, the listener hears articulated sounds, grasping them with the help of his sense organs (*indriya*). But only after the utterance is both completed and fully taken in, does its meaning become suddenly "illuminated" (*prakāśate*) in the mind of the listener. The "flashing up" (*pratibhā*), the sudden "shining out" of the intellectual intuition becomes possible only because the mind of the listener was already pregnant with the same latent word. When something is being said to us, we are not learning it for the first time—we "recognize" it as the knowledge which was already present in our own soul. In this respect the concept of "recognition" (*pratyabhijñā*),[72] suggested by Bhartṛhari and

---

71. VP, 1.84:

Nādair āhitabījāyām antyena dhvaninā saha /
Avṛttaparipākāyāṃ buddhau śabdo 'vadhāryate //

72. The very term *pratyabhijñā* first occurs in Buddhist episte-

later developed with such flourish by Kashmir Śaivites, reminds us of a similar notion of "recollection" (ἀνάμνησις) introduced by Plato.[73] The concrete and articulate sounds of ordinary speech do not originate the word's meaning; they only provide the necessary conditions that are favourable to its awakening. Incidentally, this concept of a sudden illumination of meaning helps us to understand why Bhartṛhari, in contrast to earlier grammar traditions, maintained that the meaning can be revealed only by a whole phrase, and not by each part of the sentence independently: only the completed utterance bears in

---

mological texts (in the Pali form of *paccabhiññā*), where it means a kind of knowledge attained through recognizing previously learned signs, or *abhijñā* (*abhiññā*).

73. One could remember the theory of "recollection" or "reminiscence" from Plato's dialogues *Meno* and *Phaedo*, as well as the mythological story from *Phaedrus*, according to which the soul becomes endowed with all possible wordly wisdom, while it still lingers in the divine world; however, during its strenuous journey to the earth the soul forgets most of its previous knowledge. Now it can only win it back and "remember" everything owing to constant philosophical analysis and contemplation. See Plato, *Phaedrus*, 249c-d:

> τοῦτο δ΄ἐστιν ἀνάμνησις ἐκείνον ἅ ποτ΄ εἶδεν ἡμῶν ἡ ψυχὴ συμπορευθεῖσα θεῷ καὶ ὑπεριδοῦσα ἅ νῦν εἶναί φαμεν, καὶ ἀνακύψασα εἰς τὸ ὂ ὄντως. διὸ δὴ δικαίως μόνη πτεροῦται ἡ τοῦ φιλοσόφου διάνοια· πρὸς γὰρ ἐκείνοις ἀεί ἐστιν μνήμῃ κατὰ δύναμιν, πρὸς οἷσπερ θεὸς ὤν θεῖός ἐστιν. τοῖς δὲ δὴ τοιούτοις ἀνὴρ ὑπομνήμασιν ὀρθῶς χρώμενος, τελέους ἀεὶ τελετὰς τελούμενος, τελεος ὄντως μόνος γίγνεται·

> [A]nd this is the recollection of all these things our soul once saw when it was together with God: when it was looking down from above on something that we now call being, as well as when it was looking upwards on the true being. And so, only the mind of the philosopher has wings: and it is only fair, since he is always, to the best of his abilities, clinging by his recollection to the things in which God abides, and in contemplation of which God is what he is. And whoever makes use of these memories in an appropriate way is initiated into perfect mysteries, and only he can become really perfect.

itself the reflection of the originally meaningful pattern, which is latently and safely secured in the soul of every living being.

As it is said in Bhartṛhari's treatise,

> Within this world order (*ṛte*)
>   there is no idea
>   which cannot assume
>   the form of the word;
> Every kind of knowledge shines forth,
>   being as if permeated by the word.
> If the knowledge lost
>   its constant identity
>   with the form of speech,
> Then the light would cease to clarify,
>   since it is only that [speech]
>   which makes everything
>   recognisible (*pratyavamarśinī*).[74]
>
> (*Vākya-padīya*, 1.123-24)

These *kārikās* illustrate all the key concepts of Bhartṛhari's system: here we find both the "word" (*śabda*) and "speech" (*vāk*); there is the verb "shines forth" (*bhāsate*), as well as an equally significant verb "illuminates" (*prakāśate*); and there

---

74. VP, 1.123-24:

Na so 'sti pratyayo loke yaḥ śabdānugamād ṛte /
Anuviddham iva jñānaṃ sarvaṃ śabdena bhāsate //
Vāgrūpatā ced utkrāmed avabodhasya śāśvatī /
Na prakāśaḥ prakāśeta sā hi pratyavamarśinī //

The term used here for "recognition" is a different one—*pratyavamarśa*—but this word (along with other numerous derivations of *vimarśa*, "active, powerful knowing," "knowing as energy") was as widely used by Kashmir Śaivites as *pratyabhijñāna*. For Abhinavagupta and other Śaivite authors *pratyavamarśa* was regarded as an unseparable union between two aspects of the higher consciousness, namely, as a merging together of *prakāśa* or quiet radiance of pure consciousness, and *vimarśa* or active self-awareness, which was considered to be a dynamic side of the higher Self.

is the very "shining" or "light" itself (*prakāśa*). Their correlation and interplay is traced against the background of the worldly "order" (*ṛta*)—and that provides us with an additional reason to approach everything not only from the angle of cognition but also from that of being. The author starts his argument with epistemological problems but very soon they are translated onto the ontological plane.

Later in the text we find several *kārikās* where the same idea is approached from another direction. The argument begins with the image of "speech" (*vāk*), which "enters" all living beings as an inner principle of their existence and sentience, but then states that everything eventually comes down to the "creation of meanings" (*artha-kriyā*) and the problems of cognition. As I pointed out, Bhartṛhari was discussing here one and the same process—only he considered it from two different points of view. In Bhartṛhari's own words,

> This [speech] acts as the inner consciousness
> of [living beings, caught] in *saṃsāra*,
> it stays both inside and outside.
> And no living being
> can be endowed with consciousness
> without this subtle entity.
> In order to create meanings
> speech tries to enter
> into all embodied [souls];
> If it were absent,
> everything would be insentient
> like a chunk of wood
> or a [stone] wall.[75]
>
> (*Vākya-padīya*, 126-27)

---

75. VP, 1.126-27:

Saiṣā saṃsāriṇāṃ saṃjñā bahir antaś ca vartate /
Tanmātrām avyaktikrāntaṃ caitanyaṃ sarvajātiṣu //
Arthakriyāsu vāk sarvān samīhayati dehinaḥ /
Tad utkrāntau visaṃjñeyaṃ dṛśyate kāṣṭhakuṭyavat //

It is clear, that in order to grasp this peculiar ontological entity, which is so close to the origin of all existing things, in order to "catch" the speech unawares, one needs special traps and baits, special cages where the speech would be inclined to stay and rest. In short, one needs a rare linguistical skill, one needs "the art of grammar" (*vyākaraṇa*). In my book on Śaṅkara I discussed the emergence of "figurative" or "metaphorical" (*gauṇya, aupacārika*) meaning, when poetry and hermeneutics combine their efforts in quasi-etymological investigations to show us the way towards "pure being" (or "pure consciousness"), which cannot be grasped by any other means of knowledge.[76] Of course, the entity we are keen on capturing now is not a *nirguṇa ātman* (that is, *ātman* devoid of

---

Kārikā 127 is presented as a separate *kārikā* in the edition of V. Abhyankar and Madhya Limaye. The edition of K. A. Subramania Iyer, as well as the translation of M. Biardeau, do not recognize it as a separate entrance. Hence the difference in numeration: according to the edition of V. Abhyankar and Madhya Limaye, the "Brahma-kaṇḍa," or the first chapter of the *Vākya-padīya*, is composed of 156 *kārikās*, while for K. A. Subramania Iyer and M. Biardeau there are only 155 *kārikās*.

76. See N. Isayeva, *Shankara and Indian Philosophy*, 115-23. Indeed, if *ātman* is regarded as devoid of any attributes or qualities (the way it is presented in Śaṅkara's Advaita Vedānta), if it is nothing else but a pure foundation of consciousness, it cannot really turn around to grasp its own essence, nor ever become its own object. This eternally present, unblinking gaze which comes from within, this radiance which shines forth but can never be viewed from the outside, this ray of light ever travelling in complete darkness (since there are no objects it might illuminate), is essentially ineffable, indefinable, and nothing can be said about it except the undeniable fact that it exists. Every word falls short of its target, every definition becomes false as soon as it is applied; the only possible description is that from *Bṛhadāraṇyaka Upanishad* (2.3.6 etc.): "*neti neti*"—"not thus, not thus." And still, there is something inherent in the very nature of language, something that helps to reveal reality without trying to label and bind it with an exhaustive definition; there are means of "speaking around" this pure being and consciousness, there

attributes); we are rather concerned about the Being which is, from the beginning, endowed with inner powers and creative potencies. In Bhartṛhari's system the inner link binding Being with Speech is still closer and more explicit than in Śaṅkara's Advaita Vedānta, and so the emphasis laid on language is even stronger.

According to Bhartṛhari, the original, pure Speech is not only the foundation of the whole inner structure of the universe—it is also the only base and support of all human knowledge:

---

are ways of approaching it indirectly. In Western philosophy the tradition which tried to emphasize the creative nature of language was clearly outlined by W. Humboldt, was later developed by a number of philologists and philosophers (among the most interesting was a Russian scholar who lived at the turn of the century, A. Potebnia), and was summed up in the later writings of Martin Heidegger. As Heidegger put it in one of his essays, "Der Mensch aber vermagt nur zu sprechen, insofern er, der Sage gehörend, auf sie hört, um nachsagend ein Wort sagen zu können" ("But man can only speak so far as he, while totally belonging to Speech, listens to Her and can later pronounce the word")—M. Heidegger, *Unterwegs zur Sprache* (Pfullingen, 1959), S.266. Starting with the famous declaration "Die Sprache ist der Haus des Seins" ("Language is the house of Being"), and looking for fundamental correlations between Being and Language within the fold of Greek and German etymology, Heidegger finally came to the crucial tenet: "das Wort sei Wink und nicht Zeichen in Sinne der blossen Bezeichnung" ("the word is a hint and not a sign in the sense of a mere definition")—ibid., S.119. That is, the word should be regarded as a tentative indication, as a pointer oriented towards the eternally elusive Being; it should be regarded as a symbol, inherently linked with this Being by means of its own creative power. The word in Heidegger's later writings ceases to be regarded as an arbitrary convention which is imposed on reality by general agreement, it rather becomes a self-revelation of this reality ("Die Sprache allein ist es, die eigentlich spricht. Und sie spricht einsam"—"Speech is the only one who really speaks forth. And it speaks alone"—ibid., S.265). The same line of thought can be easily traced in the hermeneutical writings of Paul Ricoeur, who always considered the words to be symbols, endowed with their own creative urge, with their own power to express and reveal reality.

This [Speech] is the foundation
of all sciences, arts and skills,
Among [the things] created
by its own power,
one thing is [always] different
from another.[77]
(*Vākya-padīya*, 1.125)

Actually, eternal Speech and the "art of grammar" are meeting here half-way: Speech willingly supports all the arts with its own inner power, while grammar "purifies" ordinary speech and helps to rid it of its fallacies. Indeed, "grammar" assumes here some of the functions usually associated with hermeneutics, since it provides everything spoken with a true interpretation. In Bhartṛhari's words,

This [grammar] is the door of liberation,
an antidote
against the faults of speech;
It purifies every kind of knowledge,
it shines forth
in [every kind of] knowledge.[78]
(*Vākya-padīya*, 1.14)

And further on he says:

It is the first stage,
[the first step] on the ladder,
which leads to perfection,
It is the straight, royal path

---

77. VP, 1.125:

Sā sarvavidyāśilpānāṃ kalānāṃ copabandhanī /
Tad vaśād api niṣpannaṃ sarvaṃ vastu vibhajyate //

78. VP, 1.14:

Tad dvāram apavargasya vāṅmalānāṃ cikitsitam /
Pavitraṃ sarvavidyānām adhividyaṃ prakāśate //

for [every person]
who thinks of liberation.[79]
(*Vākya-padīya*, 1.16)

And, finally, the same kind of a definition, presented with respect to the higher Brahman:

Though it is one,
it becomes variously divided
owing to [different] traditions;
This higher Brahman is attained
through the mastering of grammar.[80]
(*Vākya-padīya*, 1.22)

So, Speech produces both the world and the instruments of its cognition and mastering; one of the most important of these instruments is, undoubtedly, the "art of grammar." Besides the obvious role of "purifying" and "philtering" of all our utterances, grammar assumes some of the functions of literary creativity.

---

79. VP, 1.16:

Idam ādyaṃ padasthānaṃ siddhisopānaparvaṇām /
Iyaṃ sā mokṣamāṇānām ajihmā rājapaddhatiḥ //

80. VP, 1.22:

Yad ekam prakriyābhedair bahudhā pravibhajyate /
Tad vyākaraṇam āgamya paraṃ brahmādhigamyate //

9 The Stucture of the Universe and the Place of Man

The general world picture suggested by Bhartṛhari can now be briefly outlined. At the apex of the pyramid (where Śaṅkara was later to place his higher Brahman devoid of attributes—*nirguṇa-brahma*), Bhartṛhari posits Brahman, which he presents as the inner core of the Word (*śabda-tattva*, or, as it is called in somewhat later interpretations of grammar philosophy, *śabda-brahma*), or Speech (*vāk*). This Word or Speech is essentially regarded as a kind of "pulsation" or "flashing out" (*sphoṭa*), a "vibration" (*spanda*), an energy wave (*kampa*). It is known to hold within itself the infolded blossoms of "powers" (*śakti*) and potencies. Śaṅkara's Brahman is incapable of any creative impulse precisely because it is nothing but pure consciousness, which can only contemplate and look forth from within. As for Bhartṛhari's Brahman, it is swelled up from inside, it is surging by its own potencies, with the "seeds" (*bīja*) of things and meanings.[81] This Brahman is eternally pre-

---

81. Compare the plot of *La Leçon* ("The Lesson") by Eugène Ionesco. Throughout the play its main character, the teacher, is engaged in a conversation with one of his girl students, finally winding up the discussion by stabbing her with a knife. At the end of the play we suddenly realize that she is not his first victim—others seem to have been disposed of in the same manner. Theatre critics and reviewers might argue that the subject-matter of the play deals with the lack of communication between the characters, they can point out that the absurdist genre of the play does not really presuppose any rational explanation of the plot. But the heart of the matter may be entirely different. Perhaps Ionesco's parimary concern was to demon-

sent as an ever renewing net of meanings and impulses, as an energy field, which is ever intent on producing the same structures and the same outlines.

By way of yet another demonstration I could cite one more saying from Bhartṛhari's treatise—the saying which refers us back, to some of the most deep intuitions of Gauḍapāda:

> Just as in the waking state (*pravibhāge*)
> [speech], being the agent,
> acts upon the objects of action,
> In dreaming state (*avibhāge*)
> it stays on its own
> as an object of action.[82]
> (*Vākya-padīya*, 1.128)

The terms used here to determine the "waking state" (*pravibhāga*—lit., "the divided one") and the "dreaming state" (*avibhāga*, that is, "the undivided one") are somewhat unorthodox. The mention of "speech" (*vāk*) does not occur directly in Bhartṛhari's text, but I think we can implicitly rely in this interpretation on Harivṛṣabha's commentary.[83] In effect, we are

---

strate the power of language, its irresistible, invincible energy. The whole situation described in the play eventually grows out of the dialogue, where the words, desperately linking up with one another, blindly groping for one another, unavoidably bring the main character to the point when the word "knife" assumes monstrous proportions, when it becomes the only one possible, the only one existing. . . . The character is forced to act, he is pushed to action by some inner urge which is not entirely his own. Fittingly, the subject that the teacher and his student became so passionate about was grammar. Indeed, "the art of grammar" (*vyākaraṇa*) turned out to be quite a dangerous game, the outcomes and temptations of which are not always predictable.

82. VP, 1.128:

Pravibhāge yathā kartā tayā kārye pravartate /
Avibhāge tathā saiva kāryatvenāvatiṣṭhate //

83. Harivṛṣabha, "the appearance (*vivarta*) of the "Brahman-

coming back to the same fourfold matrix of being. The same set of four elements is traced in the four primordial "sounds" that constitute the sacred syllable *Oṃ*, as well as in the enumeration of the four "kinds" of speech.[84] We can see how the pattern of four points keeps recurring over and over again; what we can also discern in this pattern is the fact that the fourth point stands apart, as if embracing and subsuming the other three.

Now we come to the next problem. Why are the elements that form this net invariably four in number? Why, indeed, is the universe always modelled on this pattern? In order to answer these questions, we will have to turn to the "art of grammar," which was so highly esteemed by Bhartṛhari.

One might recall that "language," that is, pure "speech" (what F. de Saussure would call *la langue*, and not *la parole*), necessarily includes the grammatical category of "person."

Word" (*śabda-brahma*) assumes the form of things that should be done, as well as that of the means of doing them. At the moment of action in the waking state (*jāgaraṇa*), the particles of divided speech, being of the [essential] form of speech itself, attain the modifications [of gross existence] like birth, etc. and reach out towards their effects by attaining the modifications of their means. However, in the undivided states, in particular, while dreaming (*svapnādi-avibhāge*), speech itself, being devoid of objects but still assuming the nature (*svarūpa*) of external things, becomes the object of an action by attaining the modifications of their means"—"pravibhaktasādhya-sādhanarūpo hi śabdabrahmaṇo vivartaḥ / prāptajanmādivikriyā vāgvibhāgagranthayo jāgaraṇavṛttikāle vāgrūpatām anugacchanto nivṛttivikriyāprāptibhiḥ kāryeṣu yatante / svapnādyavibhāge tu saiva vāgaviṣayā bāhyavastusvarūpā satī nivṛttivikriyāprāptiṣu karmabhāvaṃ pratipadyate /"—Harivṛṣabha, *Commentary on VP*, 1.128.

84. Remember the personification of the Goddess of Speech in the form of the "sacred cow" (*gau* or *dhenu*), which is four-legged (that is, is securely placed upon four "feet," *pada*) and has an udder with four teats. Because of that, the flowing milk which feeds the whole world pours out in four distinctive streams. The image itself originates in the *Ṛg-Veda*, 8.100.10-11:

Indeed, if we try to construct the concept of Being, say, along Śaṅkara's lines, the presence of one "first person" is sufficient for this task: it is quite enough to define the place of the pure Self (*ātman*) or the pure "I." Then, to complete the picture, one can derive the third person out of this pure subject (the "third person" would, of course, represent something opposed to the notion of "I," by definition it would be a "non-I," an "*alter-Sein*" of the spirit, an external world which is located beyond the limits of my own consciousness). And for any logically consistent system (Śaṅkara was in this respect probably the most consistent of all thinkers, though virtually the same procedure was adopted in European tradition by Descartes and Fichte), this pattern of the original correspondence between

---

Yad vāg vadantyavicetanāni
  raṣṭrī devānāṃ niṣasāda mandrā /
Catasra ūrjaṃ duduhe payāṃsi
  kva svid asyāḥ paramaṃ jagāma //
Devīṃ vācam ajanayanta devās tāṃ
  viśvarūpāḥ paśavo vadanti /
Sā no mandreṣam urjaṃ duhānā
  dhenur vāg asmān upa suṣṭutaitu //

When the resounding Speech,
  the sweet-sounding
  Mistress of the gods,
  came down
  to the mindless [creatures,]
She allowed herself to be milked
  [to provide] nourishment and milk
  in four [separate flows].
  Whither [then]
  came her best part?
The gods praise the goddess Speech,
  so it is said,
  by multi-formed creatures.
The sweet-sounding milk-cow,
  who gives us nourishment and milk,
  be thou praised, oh Speech,
  that comes down to us!

"I" and "non-I" is enough. One should bear in mind, of course, that the pronoun "I" is used here as a pure abstraction, without any reference to its possible psychological connotations; in accordance with the tenets of linguistics (say, on the lines suggested by É. Benveniste or R. Barthes) it is taken as a mere designation for an absolute subject, for the "first person." It essentially indicates the initial point of perception and reasoning, presenting an appropriate grammar category to refer to the "speaker," the "addressant," the starting point of all reasoning and perception. Then the "non-I," the "he" or "it," is regarded primarily as something standing in absolute opposition to this subject; the "third person" always refers to the object of consideration, to the "object" par excellence—and it does not matter whether we regard it as something really existing or whether, having denied its reality, we regard it as being dependent upon and derived from the ultimate subject, the Self.

However, we get quite a different picture as soon as we try to locate the source of universe and existence in Speech. Speech itself (representing the absolute "I," the absolute "first person" within a grammar paradigm) certainly speaks "of"

Finally, as it is put in another *Ṛg-Veda* hymn (1.164.45),

Speech is measured
by four quarters
known to the sage brahmans.
Three of them remain concealed
and are not manifested,
while the fourth one
is used for speaking
by human beings.

Catvāri vāk parimitā padāni tāni
vidur brāhmaṇā ye manīṣiṇaḥ /
Guha trīṇi nihita neṅgayanti
turīyaṃ vāco manuṣyā vadanti //

Note that here the "fourth" state (*turīya*) is presented as the one spoken by "human beings," which is a clear indication of the interchangeability of the names (even the most sacred ones). What remains intact in any case is the pattern, the fourfold division itself.

something, "about" something (about "him" or "it," that is, ultimately, about the "third person" of grammar). Nevertheless, it is equally important that Speech cannot speak without addressing itself to someone (to some absolute "you" or "thou," to an "addressee," to the "second person"). As it was shown by Émile Benveniste, the real opposition, the real abyss separates two absolute "persons" (that is, "me" and "you") from an absolute non-personal "him" or "it." The "third person" is essentially absent when the conversation is taking place; the "non-person," the "absent one," is "somebody" reduced to being "something"—that is, reduced to being nothing but the object of the conversation. And while the discourse, the conversation is going on, the two participants engaged in the dialogue are mutually reversible in their respective positions: when they address each other (and as long as they continue to address each other), they keep changing places, taking alternate turns in accepting the indicated positions of being the "addressant" and the "addressee." In contrast to that, from the point of view of grammar theory, the absolute "non-person" ("he," "she," "it") cannot ever become sentient and endowed with words, cannot ever, so to speak, turn to face us.[85]

The emergence of this absolute "you" or "thou," the emergence of the "second person" immediately leads us beyond the limits of a purely logical system of thought. It presupposes the dialogue, presupposes other person's sentiency and reality, presupposes the multitude of souls, as well as the God who has a form and a face, the God, magnificently capable of addressing us.

Coming back to the subject at hand, we can easily see that in the Vedānta of Gauḍapāda and Bhartṛhari the level of the grammatical "third person" is that of the world, of the universe (*viśva*) which is perceived in the "waking state" (*jāgarita*). It is the plane of existence when we believe that our perceptions originate from the external objects; and, simul-

---

85. See Émile Benveniste, *Problèmes de linguistique générale* (Paris: Gallimard, 1974), vol. 2, 202-3, 213-14 (the chapter entitled: "L'antonyme et le pronom en français moderne").

taneously, it is the stage of "manifested" (*vaikharī*) speech, of speech which finds its support and embodiment in a quasi-material substrate of empirical, articulated sounds (*nāda*). The level of the absolute "second person" is the level of actually existing individual souls, of separate, "shining" (*taijasa*) points of consciousness that are capable of producing images, dreams, and illusions out of their own inner nature, even in the absence of any empirical objects. At the same time, it is the stage of "middle" (*madhyamā*) speech, which inwardly persists in creating its own mental images. And, finally, the absolute "first person," the "I," the absolute "grammatical subject" is presented by the "conscious" (*prājña*) *ātman* in the state of deep sleep (*supta*), when the *ātman* returns to its inner essence, shedding all external attributes. It is also the level of "seeing" (*paśyantī*) speech, speech which is concentrated in a single, indivisible "point" of contemplation. The "fourth" state embraces them all, sustaining them within itself; the first three stages are retained inside as a suppressed spring ready to be released, as a folded blossom on the verge of opening, as a highly condensed node or "drop" (*bindu*) of energy, as an innermost "seed" (*bīja*) of potency.

This is why the path leading us from these versions of Vedānta to the openly theistical tenets of the Tāntrikas, runs so smoothly. It is from this fourfold construction that Gauḍapāda's mention of *asparśa-yoga* ("yoga devoid of any relations") eventually stems; this concept forms a natural enough bridge between Bhartṛhari's grammar teaching and the mystical revelations of Kashmir Śaivism. Śaṅkara's Advaita did not concern itself with the problem of the correlation between the absolute "I" and the absolute "you"; it became indifferent to the relationship between God and the individual soul, relegating it to the sphere of "profane," "lower" knowledge (*apara-vidyā*). Even before Śaṅkara's time, however, the Vedānta of his predecessors, with their emphasis on speech itself, on the fourfold matrix of being, quite consistently shifted the interest of their followers towards the theme of divine worship, towards the problem of God's mercy and omnipotence, as well as towards the recognition of the importance of the sacred tradition (*āgama*, *āmnaya*) and Vedic injunctions.

Incidentally, this approach to the Vedānta of Bhartṛhari and Gauḍapāda sheds light on another point, the source of much confusion in Vedānta philosophy.

It is well known that both Pūrva-Mīmāṃsā and Vedānta were noted for their unwavering reliance on the Vedas, for their highly pious attitude towards sacred scripture.[86] However, while demonstrating their veneration to the whole of the texts of the Veda canon, the Mīmāṃsākas demonstrated their preference for the Vedic "injunctions" (*vidhi*), that is, for the direct commands, usually connected with ritual, found in the Vedic texts. Śaṅkara, on the contrary, clearly preferred "explanatory" sayings (the so-called *arthavāda* sayings), passages full of metaphors, connotations, parables, and other literary devices of "indirect" (*parokṣa*) communication. Moreover, Śaṅkara's own works (and he was undoubtedly not only the greatest philosopher but one of the greatest Indian poets of his time) were, to a great extent, modelled after these texts.[87]

One would expect that Bhartṛhari, with his keen attention to language and his veneration of highly mythologized Speech, would be a direct predecessor of Śaṅkara in recognizing the prevalence of *arthavāda* sayings. Yet everything was exactly the other way round: Bhartṛhari fully agreed with the tenets of Mīmāṃsā followers in giving priority to the *vidhi* formulas. But the whole situation is seen in a different light as soon as we remember that Speech, or the absolute "first person," the absolute subject, is ever looking for a personal counterpart, search-

---

86. The concept of *veda-mūlatva*, or the notion according to which the Vedas constitute the "root" (*mūla*), the foundation of all worldly knowledge and learning. It was mainly propounded by the Mīmāṃsā teachers, but later on became an important cornerstone in Śaṅkara's Vedānta. See Jaimini, *Mīmāṃsā-sūtra*, 1.1.2.

87. In his polemics with the followers of Mīmāṃsā, Śaṅkara places them on the same level with the so-called "dry logicians" (*śuṣka-tarka-vādinaḥ*), who allegedly could not use the language and its inherent poetical or symbolical potential to the full extent. See Śaṅkara, *Commentary on "Brahma-sūtra,"* 2.1.11, 2.2.6, etc.

ing for an absolute "you" or "thou," in other words, for somebody to address. So the Vedic "injunctions" (*vidhi*) have a unique role to play in this relationship: like biblical commandments, they become a "call," an "appeal" of Speech; they essentially manifest its effort to arrest or draw the attention of the potential "addressee."

The injunctions (or "prohibitions"—*pratiṣedha*—which constitute a kind of "reverse side" for the *vidhi* sayings) are not important for their contents (after all, they often urge us to ascribe moral values or moral motivations to an indifferent and complicated ritual action). However, as soon as I agree to recognize their authority, as soon as I agree to become "enjoinable," I immediately lose my indifferent and disinterested stand of being a mere stranger and assume the position of an "addressee," the position of a rightful participant in the dialogue. Instead of being an outsider, I assume the role of the "second person," thus becoming an absolute "you," a listening "thou," an addressee for the message of Speech, while Speech, in its turn, recognizes me as a subject and agrees to become a similar "second person," a similar absolute "you," "thou," or an "addressee" in our mutual relationship. And that signifies the beginning of a real dialogue, the emerging possibility of an exchange of energies, and eventually a reiteration, a recreation of the original "flashing up" of the primordial fourfold net.

We might even maintain that, for Śaṅkara, poetical creativity or philosophical invention was essentially a "reflection" of the play of *māyā*, and the ultimate goal was to make the reflecting mirror itself not only clear but positively translucent, so that the inner light of *ātman* could shine through it unimpeded. Meanwhile, one could say that both Gauḍapāda and Bhartṛhari were primarily concerned with turning poetical or philosophical creativity into a form of "participation" in the divine play of creation, into an ontologically necessary and inescapable replay of the perpetual oscillation of the primordial energy pattern. And Bhartṛhari's own *vyākaraṇa* or "art of grammar" reminds us not so much of the elaborate and minute grammar discussions of Pāṇini or Patañjali, but rather of a genuine creative effort of an artist or a poet.

III Further Developments: The Interplay of Energies and Artistic Creation

10 Early Vedānta and Kashmir Śaivism

According to early Vedānta, the form of the existing universe is set in advance by a structure-producing matrix, which is essentially fourfold. Also, there are reasons to believe that this matrix is closely related to primordial Speech (*vāk*) or the Word (*śabda*). At least, one can clearly discern in it the pulsation and reverberation of some initial "sound."

Both in the grammar system of Bhartṛhari and in the Advaita Vedānta teaching of Gauḍapāda, the problem of "pure Brahman" (*nirguṇa-brahma*, that is, Brahman devoid of attributes) is, so to speak, put into parenthesis. What we encounter instead at the apex of the pyramid of being is an extraordinary language (or sound) entity, the symbol of which—as well as one of the possible ways of approaching it—is given to us in the form of the sacred syllable *Oṃ*. This resounding wave of energy, this entity, is fourfold. Its four constituent sounds or elements create the same fourfold pattern everywhere, either as recurring patterns of consciousness or as fundamental structures of the universe. Yet the elements themselves are neither real nor unreal. The only reality is that of an inner surge of energy which reverberates with its own peculiar rhythm.

This explains why, when talking about Brahman, both Vedāntins use similar terms or derivations from the same word-root. In their discussions of the higher Brahman, the same words crop up: *spanda*, *sphoṭa*, *sphuṭa*, *sphurattā*, *kampa*, all of them conveying the same meaning of perpetual "vibration," "pulsation," "shimmering." The whole universe is evoked by the pulsation of this field, which is ever oscillating between alternating states of expansion (manifestation) and contraction.

Here we shall consider how this early Vedāntic worldview evolved in later Vedānta and in Kashmir Śaivism. Basically, there were two possibilities open for early Vedānta: the first one was later moulded into Śaṅkara's version of Advaita, while the second was naturally developed in the ideas of Kashmir Śaivism.[1] In both cases the main problem was to find a plausible and satisfactory link between the higher Brahman and the created universe. The main difficulty was to bridge the gap between God, as the only one real entity, and the multitude of created beings.

For Śaṅkara, the solution was quite a drastic one: according to his version of Advaita Vedānta, creation was something that never happened, and the existing multitude of beings was just an illusory appearance. In Śaṅkara's Advaita the higher Brahman is regarded as essentially ineffable (*anirvacanīya*), devoid of qualities or attributes (*nirguṇa*), as something that stays beyond any possibility of evolution (*apariṇāma*) and is nothing but pure consciousness itself (*caitanya, vidyā*). For non-dualist Kashmir Śaivites, however, the higher Brahman is already full of inner potencies and powers (*śakti*) and is evolving into the multitude of the created uni-

---

1. Whenever I make use here of this much too broad and general definition, I mainly follow the approach of André Padoux, who referred to "what is usually, but not very felicitously, called 'Kashmir Śaivism,' that is to say, in fact, to the various nondualistic Śaiva (or Śaktaśaiva) traditions, which emerged, developed, and flourished most brilliantly in Kashmir, or which are traditionally associated with this region" (André Padoux, *Vāc: The Concept of the Word in Selected Hindu Tantras* [Albany: SUNY Press, 1990]). Padoux gives in his book a very lucid and succinct presentation of the history of Kashmir Śaivism and its literature. The best general essay and analytical classification of Kashmir Śaivism is, probably, that of Alexis Sanderson ("Śaivism and the Tantric Tradition," in S. Sutherland and others (eds.), *The World's Religions* [London: Routledge, 1988]), 660-704.

verse through a series of self-transformations (*pariṇāma*).

The link between Gauḍapāda and Bhartṛhari, on the one hand, and the Kashmir Śaivites, on the other, is certainly much more evident and natural than any linkes that might exist between these early Vedāntins and Śaṅkara's Advaita Vedānta. It is well known, for instance, that one of the greatest philosophers and aestheticians of Kashmir, Abhinavagupta, in his treatise *Tantra-āloka* ("The Light of Tantra") often makes direct reference to the grammar theories of Bhartṛhari. It is maintained in the treatise that the followers of the "grammar tradition" recognize "Brahman as the Word" (*śabda-brahma*) to be the higher reality, and that this Brahman is considered to be essentially identical with the "seeing" (*paśyantī*) Speech.[2]

The closest parallels to Gauḍapāda's and Bhartṛhari's ideas are to be found mainly within the fold of so-called nondualist Śaivism. The religious foundation for it was primarily secured by the schools of Trika (the concept of adoration of the three goddesses of the trident) and Krama (the concept of a gradual descent, stepping down of the divine power),[3] while the philosophical notions were supplied by the elaborate theoretical constructions of the schools of Spanda and Pratyabhijñā.

Spanda literally means "pulsation," "vibration"; this philosophical school of Kashmir Śaivism became fully shaped and developed as early as the ninth century. By that time two of its basic texts (*Śiva-sūtra* or "The Sūtras of Śiva," regarded as the Lord's own reveleation bestowed on the sage Vasugupta,

---

2. And even though for Abhinavagupta the main fault of Bhartṛhari's system lies with the assumption of this "seeing" (*paśyantī*) Speech as the highest possible entity (since the Śaivite philosopher was, of course, opting for the "higher Speech" (*parā vāk*) as the source and foundation of all universe), he still addresses Bhartṛhari with a honorific title, calling him *tatrabhavān* ("that [esteemed] master," "that lord").

3. With the possible addition of the so-called Parā religious trend, or the cult of the "Higher [Goddess]," which became quite prominent in the later works of Abhinavagupta.

and *Spanda-kārikā*, "The Kārikās on Vibration," composed by Vasugupta, or, possibly, by his disciple Kallaṭa) already started to enjoy prominence and authority. In the words of Alexis Sanderson, this school presents Śiva as "all-inclusive reality, a single, unified consciousness, which manifests itself in all subjects, acts and objects of experience by virtue of an inherent and infinite dynamism."[4] It is quite easy to see that this "dynamism" or eternal "vibration" bears a curious resemblance to the "pulsation" which constitutes the only foundation of reality and consciousness in some of the schools of early Vedānta philosophy.

From the beginning of the tenth century the Spanda school starts to undergo certain inner changes. The work *Śiva-dṛṣṭi* ("The Seeing of Śiva") by Somānanda virtually paved the way for the development of the new trend, which somewhat later came to be known as the Pratyabhijñā school of non-dualist Kashmir Śaivism. As it was with the Spanda school, the very name of Pratyabhijñā immediately refers us back to some of the key ideas of Bhartṛhari's teaching. As we mentioned earlier, in Bhartṛhari's treatise *pratyabhijñā* means "recognition"; it implies the "recollection" or "reminiscence" of some important knowledge which is already latent in the adept's consciousness, but must be specially elicited and "recognized" as the higher reality, as something that brings him closer to Brahman. According to the tenets of non-dualist Kashmir Śaivism, Śiva himself has to be "recognized" as that inner entity within the heart of the adept (*sādhaka*) which constitutes not only the foundation of his consciousness but also the ultimate promise of liberation.[5]

The initial point for the emergence of this new school is usually defined by the text *Īśvara-pratyabhijñā-kārikā* ("The

---

4. Alexis Sanderson, "Śaivism and the Tantric Traditions," 694.

5. In a striking simile found in one of the Śaivite texts, Śiva keeps coming to the soul as an unknown, dark lover who only after some time becomes gradually "recognized" and accepted; only then the real merging together becomes possible, and the soul "melts away" (*vilīyate*) into Śiva's entity.

Kārikās on the Recognition of the Lord"), composed in the beginning of the tenth century by Somānanda's son and disciple, Utpaladeva. Utpaladeva wrote his own commentary on this basic text (*Vivṛti*), but its most important interpretation was given by one of Utpaladeva's later followers, Abhinavagupta (late tenth to early eleventh century). Besides commenting upon Utpaladeva's treatise (*Īśvara-pratyabhijñā-vimarśinī*) and upon Utpaladeva's auto-commentary (*Īśvara-pratyabhijñā-vivṛti-vimarśinī*), Abhinavagupta composed a number of other philosophical texts; the most significant among the latter were *Tantra-sāra* ("The Essence of Tantra"), *Tantra-āloka* ("The Light of Tantra"), and *Parā-triṃśikā-vivaraṇa* ("The Commentary on the Thirty[-six Ślokas] about the Higher [Goddess]"). And, last but not least, he left several works on aesthetics, literary and dramatic theory which, curiously enough, in many respects stand even closer to the ideas of early Vedānta than his metaphysical compositions.

Propounding the ideas of the Pratyabhijñā school of thought, its followers, notably Abhinavagupta, regarded themselves as thinkers who achieved some kind of synthesis which eventually succeeded in embracing earlier non-dualist Śaivite notions. Abhinavagupta's closest disciple, Kṣemarāja (eleventh century) wrote an authoritative commentary on *Spanda-kārikā*, and Abhinavagupta himself felt that he was more of a follower of the ideas of his predecessors than their staunch opponent and critic. In other words, the two basic notions of *spanda* and *pratyabhijñā*, which remind us so strongly of early Vedānta tenets, became equally relevant, equally prominent in Abhinavagupta's teaching.

Actually, the main idea, shared by all schools of thought within the fold of non-dualist Kashmir Śaivism, was that of the cosmic union between two entities (or, rather, between two aspects of one and the same indivisible entity—the conscious and the active one—personified, respectively, by the figures of Śiva and his loving consort Śakti. As it is said in Abhinavagupta's *Parā-triṃśikā-vivaraṇa*, "it is impossible to conceive any difference, which could [separate] Śakti from

Śiva."[6] At the same time, this union is an expression of the two aspects of consciousness: on the one hand, consciousness is the pure, quiet light of contemplation (*prakāśa*), symbolized by Śiva; while, on the other, consciousness is already endowed with a whole range of inner potencies, with the dynamic self-awareness as the "will to know," with the inner urge to transgress its own limits (this aspect is called *vimarśa* and is represented by the inner dynamism of Śakti). And it is this dynamic, ever evolving aspect of the reality, which comes to be identified with "Speech" (*vāk*), ever present at the source and origin of every creation.

For Utpaladeva this "power" (*śakti*) or "energy" of the higher Speech has already assumed the form of a self-reflecting, self-discerning pulsating consciousness (*ahaṃ-pratyavamarśa*), while Abhinavagupta, in turn, supplied a subtle link between the dynamic urge of "self-reflection" (*vimarśa*) and a quasi-erotic mysticism of the energies of the "heart" (*hṛdaya*). In any case, as Mark Dyczkowski puts it, practically all nondualist schools of Kashmir Śaivism "share a basic vision of ultimate reality as a single creative-cum-destructive dynamic, divine consciousness."[7]

This union or intermingling of two universal entities, is conceived as a constant "vibration," "pulsation," or inner "throb" (*spanda*, *sphurattā*),[8] which becomes the foundation for the evolution of the created world. This flashing forth,

---

6. "na hi śaktiḥ śivād bhedam āmarśayet"—Abhinavagupta, *Parā-triṃśikā-vivaraṇa* (Srinagar, 1918), 3.

7. See *The Stanzas on Vibration*, translated with introduction and exposition by Mark S. G. Dyczkowski (Albany: SUNY Press, 1992), 38.

8. Abhinavagupta adds to this string of synonyms, all of which convey the same meaning of something "shining through," something reverberating and radiating forth, yet another term: *ullāsa* or "exuberant joy," "cheerful play" (sometimes it might even mean a dissolute "dancing"). To some extent it was a tribute to the profound erotic significance of the interplay between Śiva and Śakti—an aspect, which was extremely important for all Tāntric schools. Partly,

which is simultaneously construed as a manifestation of primordial Speech, gradually condenses and darkens in its descent downwards; it is gradually transformed and ultimately moulded into the manifold universe of created objects. But since the initial movement of consciousness is present in every human being, the task of the adept (*sādhaka*) is to contemplate this union, to experience it directly in the "flashing out" (*prathibhā*) of mystical illumination, or, in the terms of the Pratyabhijñā school of Kashmir Śaivism, to "recognize" himself as identical with the higher Lord.

In Utpaladeva's metric treatise *Īśvara-pratyabhijñā-kārikā*, it is put in the following way:

> Since *ātman* cannot be called
> an unconscious one,
> it is proclaimed to be
> consciousness itself;
> And this [consciousness], in its turn,
> is identical with activity,
> owing to which we can
> distinguish it
> from inanimate things.
> The essence of this active consciousness
> is to be conscious of oneself.
> The higher speech is ever manifested
> through itself.
> It is truly the self-sufficiency,
> the higher lordship
> of the higher *ātman*.
> This consciousness is a shimmering vibration,
> the higher reality
> which lies beyond
> the time and the space.
> While constituting
> the inner essence [of Brahman],

---

however, the word refers us to the aesthetical theory of poetics propounded by Abhinavagupta.

it is also called
the heart of the great Lord.[9]
(Utpaladeva, *Īśvara-pratyabhijñā-kārikā*, 1.5.12-14)

First of all, we should note some striking terminological similarities. It is certainly not coincidental that right here, next to the primordial source of the universe, we find the idea of the "higher speech" (*parā vāk*), which was so prominent if not in Bhartṛhari's treatise itself, then at least in Harvṛṣabha's commentary on *Vākyapadīya*. In his gloss on Utpaladeva's text, Abhinavagupta suggests his own interpretation of this notion. In his words,

> this consciousness (*pratyavamarśa*) is called the speaking out (*śabdana*) which has the nature of inner expression. This speaking verily has nothing to do with [ordinary] conventional language (*saṅketa*). It is the act of radiant bliss, similar to an inner nod [of agreement]. It is something that gives life to the letters and other [things], it is also the [inner] form of [ordinary] conventional words on the level of *māyā*, since it is the foundation of all other representations. . . . This [speech] is called "the higher one" becvause of its fullness, and it is called "speech" (*vāk*) because it speaks (*vakti*), giving a verbal expression to all the universe owing to this representation. Because of this we can say that [Speech] is created and spoken by itself, since it is essentially consciousness (*cidrūpatā*), that is, it is rooted in its own being—eternally existing [consciousness] of "I."[10]

---

9. Utpaladeva, *Īśvara-pratyabhijñā-kārikā*, 1.5.12-14:

Ātmataiva caitanyaṃ citkriyā citikartṛtā /
Tatparyeṇoditas tena jaḍāt sa hi vilakṣaṇaḥ //
Citiḥ pratyavamarśātmā parā vāksvarasoditā /
Svātantryam etanmukhyaṃ tadaiśvaryaṃ paramātmanaḥ //
Sā sphurattā mahāsattā deśakālāviśeṣiṇī /
Saiṣā sāratayā proktā hṛdayaṃ parameṣṭhiṇaḥ //

10. Abhinavagupta, *Īśvara-pratyabhijñā-vimarśinī*, 1.5.13:

With this idea of energy, this concept of vibration of consciousness and speech, now part of the very core of the higher entity, the followers of the Pratyabhijñā school of Kashmir Śaivism established the possibility of a new approach to the cosmic manifestations of Brahman. These manifestations are no longer regarded on a par with Śaṅkara's illusory worldly phenomena that appear to be "superimposed" ('adhyasyate') upon the unchangeable reality of the higher Brahman. But neither are they considered to be the effects of an independently evolving entity similar to the *prakṛti* of the Sāṃkhyayikas. The cosmic aspects and manifestations are nothing but latent possibilities, actually present, actually inherent within the "heart" (*hṛdaya*) of Brahman; these possibilities are capable of a sudden "flashing up," of a sudden "splitting up" into a multitude of perceptible objects. The same continuation of the ideas is evident in the very choice of terms: the Śaiva, Tāntric in its essence, *sphurattā* ("bright, intermittent flashing out," "brilliance") is, of course, quite close to Bhartṛhari's and Harivṛṣabha's *sphoṭa*, *sphuṭa*, and *sphurattā*. And the idea of the four stages of primordial Speech, so important in Abhinavagupta's system, is even more consistent and elaborate than its counterpart found in a much earlier version of the same concept suggested by the *Vākya-padīya*.

Even Gauḍapāda's idea of *turīya* has a direct correspondence in Abhinavagupta's later works. In his brief metric treatise *Paramārtha-sāra* ("The Essence of the Higher Truth"), he writes:

> Creation, maintenance, and dissolution,
> as well as the states of waking, dreaming,
> and deep sleep,

"Pratyavamarśaś ca antarabhilāpātmakaśabdanasvabhavaḥ tac ca śabdanaṃ saṅketanirapekṣam eva avicchinnacamatkārātmakam antarmukhaśironirdeśaprākhyam akārādimāyīyasāṅketikaśabdajīvitabhūtam . . . pratyavamarśāntarbhittibhūtatvāt pūrṇatvāt parā vakti viśvam abhilāpati pratyavamarśena iti ca vāk ata eva sā svarasena cidrūpatayā svātmaviśrāntivapuṣā uditā sadānastamitā nityā aham ity eva /"

Are all shining forth
inside the "fourth" [state] (*turīya*),
which shines forth [in its turn],
without being obstructed by them.
The "waking" [state] is the "universal" one,
owing to the differences [within it];
the "dreaming" [state] is the "shining" one,
because it reveals its nature as light;
And the [state] of the "deep sleep"
is [called] the "conscious" one,
since it is [nothing but] the lump of
consciousness.
But the "fourth" (*turīya*) one
is higher than all this . . .
Through the application
of the trident of his powers,[11]
all of this [universe] is set forth
By the Lord of gods
who [is known] by the name of Śiva
inside his lordly [abode],
inside the higher truth.[12]

(*Paramārtha-sāra*, 34-35, 45)

However, we should not let all these astonishing similarities obscure the differences between Bhartṛhari's teaching and

11. The "powers" (*śaktayaḥ*) of the higher Lord are his *icchā-śakti* ("the power of will"), *jñāna-śakti* ("the power of consciousness") and *kriyā-śakti* ("the power of action"). All of them can to some extent be identified with the "power of Speech" (*vāk*) that desires, cognizes, and brings forth the world.

12. Abhinavagupta, *Paramārtha-sāra*, 34-35, 45:

Sṛṣṭisthitisaṃhārā jāgratsvapnau suṣuptam iti tasmin /
Bhānti turīye dhāmani tathāpi tair nāvṛtaṃ bhāti //
Jāgradviśvaṃ bhedāt svapnas tejaḥ prakāśamāhātmyāt /
Prājñaḥ suptāvasthā jñānaghanatvāt tataḥ paraṃ turyam // . . .
Śaktitriśūlaparigamayogena samastham api parameśe /
Śivanāmani paramārthe visṛjyate devadevena //

the tenets of the Kashmir Śaivites. In fact, the discrepancies become clear when we take a closer look at Tāntric philosophy. In the third chapter of Abhinavagupta's treatise *Tantra-āloka* we find the image of the gradual evolution of the divine power into the world. "Mother Śakti" is undergoing transformations and evolving into the created universe through a series of intermediate stages. It creates the world while itself assuming the various forms of the sounds and the letters of the Sanskrit alphabet. The vowels and the consonants are represented as manifold variations of an inner vibration which is inherent in Śiva's own consciousness; at the same time, they are presumed to be actually existing in the form of definitely shaped and fixed stages in the gradual creation (*sṛṣṭi*) of the external world.[13]

One could argue that some of these possibilities were already present in Bhartṛhari's *Vākya-padīya*, where, as we remember, the higher entity is referred to in the following way:

> And this one and only [Brahman],
> this seed of all [existing things],
> already has the distinction
> In the form of the perceiving [subject],
> that of the perceived [object],
> as well as the perception itself.[14]
> (*Vākya-padīya*, 1.4)

Nevertheless, a distinguishing trait of Bhartṛhari's and Gauḍapāda's treatises is their refusal to commit themselves to rigid definitions. Everything there is still fluid, still oscillating between *nirguṇa* and *saguṇa* ideas. At the point where the Kashmir Śaivites would rather suggest a quasi-Neoplatonic version of creation with its gradual descent, splitting up, and

---

13. See Abhinavagupta, *Tantra-āloka*, 154-56.

14. Bhartṛhari, *Vākya-padīya*, 1.4:

Ekasya sarvabījasya yasya ceyamanekadhā /
Bhoktṛbhoktavyarūpeṇa bhogarūpeṇa ca sthitiḥ //

ultimate diminishing of the initial light, the early Vedāntins clearly demonstrate their inclination towards reasoning on the level of energies. Instead of the condensing of the initial luminuosity, which continues on and on, until finally achieving the form of the real objects, early Vedānta suggests a continuous oscillation, a continuous shimmering of the primordial pattern.

According to Śaṅkara's Advaita, nothing at all happens to the higher Brahman, creation itself is illusory—it simply does not exist as an ontological reality. In contrast to that, from the point of view of non-dualist Kashmir Śaivism, what happens after the initial outburst of the vibrating energy is the real process of creation, which starts as a kind of perpetual emanation of forms and objects—and these forms and objects tend to freeze into rigid hierarchies of being. Meanwhile, in early Vedānta (at least in the versions presented by Gauḍapāda and Bhartṛhari) the initial energy finds itself an expression in a series of fleeting, oscillating images, in the process of naming, in the voice devoid of any material embodiment, in the recurrent outline and reiterated structure which is being born over and over again.

The Tāntric Śaiva philosophers began their argument with the same concept of the primordial light, which is regarded as essentially filled with its own urges and potencies, bursting forth in its own creative effort. However, according to them, this initial emanation of light becomes trapped and condensed, it is slowed down in its gradual procession; while taking a sequence of steps, it assumes on its way down various intermediate shapes and forms in a multilayered hierarchy of existence.[15] And the same rigid hierarchies can be traced in the stages of the adept's way, when he starts his movement in the opposite direction, when he tries to concentrate on this initial

---

15. Kashmir Śaivites were quite prolific in their efforts to establish and elaborate very complicated hierarchies of being, that is, of gradual descent of the "higher speech," and its gradual transformation into a tangible and visible world. Of course, the concrete examples, as well as the concrete order or creation differ from school to school. But generally one can determine this "descent" in the following way.

point (*bindu*) of the light of consciousness. As André Padoux puts it, "this cosmic movement, in a Tāntric system of thought, has its microcosmic counterpart, both being linked through constant correspondences and interrelations, so that the movement toward creation appears as that which creates human bondage, and the movement of withdrawal as that of deliverance."[16] Hence all the elaborate schemes and intricate structures presented by the Kashmir philosophers, hence all their attempts to describe the correspondences between different phenomena of the perceptible world, and their respective counterparts (or prototypes) in the higher, "divine" worlds.

Everything begins with the higher consciousness which is, at the same time, a union of two aspects: a quiet, passive, contemplative light (*prakāśa*) and a dynamic, active self-reflection (*vimarśa*). Their union (which is usually understood as the level of *parā vāk*, or the "higher speech") gives birth to a primordial, yet inaudible sound (*nāda*), which becomes concentrated in a "drop" or "point" (*bindu*) of phonic energy. Then the initial driving force within Speech brings it to the level of "seeing" (*paśyantī*) speech, and starts to unfold further, producing first the ideal matrix, the ideal united conglomerate of all the phonemes (*mātṛka*, or the "mother" of real creation, which corresponds to the level of the "middle," *madhyamā*, speech), and later the actual articulated phonemes themselves, along with the words and sayings—and together with the whole of the created universe (the level of "manifested" or "corporeal"—*vaikharī*—speech).

16. See André Padoux, *Vāc*, 82.

11 The Concept of Energies: Neoplatonist and Hesychast Parallels

Now, let us see what happens when the higher entity is envisaged as something actually emanating into the world, as something splitting into a multitude of countless manifestations. What becomes easily recognizable here in a series of inevitable theoretical developments is their quasi-Neoplatonic intent, which eventually comes into play and colors the emerging ontological picture in its own hues.

On the one hand, it invariably calls for the construction of elaborate and rigid hierarchies that are expected to provide intermediate links, bridging together the "one and only" immovable entity on the apex of the pyramid with the changing phenomenal world at the bottom. On the other hand, it has certain pronounced dualistic implications, since the very emanation or the splitting up of the initial principle is usually considered to be taking place within some dense and resisting media. In other words, even if "matter," which provides the receptacle for the process of creation, is essentially presented as a mere negation, it is still regarded as an opposing principle, as something definitely dangerous and alien, as some kind of a dark background, which is ultimately responsible for the refraction and weakening of the initial light. That is why, for instance, Christian Neoplatonics (even the most venerated sages like Origen or Evagrius Pontius) could never totally escape the stigma of potentially dualistic implications, the suspicion of an Arrian or Manichean heresy. And that is why most of the Tāntric Śaiva and Vaiṣṇava schools (including all the supposedly non-dualistic Śaiva schools, and even Abhinavagupta's branch of the Pratyabhijñā school) were clearly drifting away from Śaṅkara's monism and tending towards potentially dualistic creeds and notions.

Meanwhile, for Gauḍapāda and Bhartṛhari the solution of the problem of "one" and "many" aspects of Brahman was to be sought on the level of energies. At the same time, this problem was closely intertwined with the notion of "speech," or, at least, with the concept of some peculiar resounding, phonic power, with the inner force of language, that is, with the alleged power of poetry and grammar to reveal and unfold their own inherent meanings. And while Kasmir Śaivites regarded Speech (*vāk*) and the Word (*śabda*) as a flowing emanation, capable of bringing about real "creation" (*sṛṣṭi*), Bhartṛhari was far more concerned about the ability of speech to express meanings. Curiously enough, this aspect of Bhartṛhari's grammar system seems to be much more consistently followed not in Abhinavagupta's ontological theories, but rather in the latter's aesthetical ideas, especially in the idea of *dhvani* as "evoked," "implied," or "suggested" meaning—the meaning which cannot ever be pinpointed and explained. According to the Abhinavagupta's aesthetics, *dhvani* undoubtedly exists, even though it lacks an actual embodiment; it exists only as an elusive and ineffable hint, an unmanifested pattern that can be "recognized" in the solid conglomerate words and sentences already endowed with a definite literal sense.

In my study of the history of Western philosophy and religion I could find only one close correlation with this kind of approach: the analogy appears in one of the trends in Eastern Orthodox spirituality. Curiously enough, it is a sect which was often branded as "Christian yoga,"[17] though the designation had no ontological implications and was primarily suggested

---

17. See Jean Meiendorff, *Introduction à l'étude de Gregoire Palamas* (Paris: De Seuil, 1959), 134-38. The very concept of the "intellectual prayer," based on silent contemplation (ἡσυχία), was introduced by Gregory of Nyssa and Nicephor Hesychast in the fourth century and later developed by Evagrius Pontius. The con-

due to the employment of some peculiar exercises in prayer and Christian meditation. The sect I have in mind is that of the Hesychasts, originally the monks from the Mount Athos who were famous for practising ἡσυχία (lit., "silence," "deep concentration"). The practice in question included the constant and silent repetition of the so-called Jesus prayer—a short, rigid, and unchangeable chant used almost like a mantra. The words of the prayer were repeated over and over again, until they were finally brought into resonance with the inner rhythms of the body, especially with the rhythm of the adept's breathing. After that, even the words themselves became unnecessary and superfluous, and the fully interiorized prayer continued its inner life within the deepest core of the adept's being.

However, it is not the practice of monastic contemplation that compels our interest when we draw parallels between early Vedānta and some Christian concepts. Spiritual practice and mythological images are of no use in comparative discussion if we do not understand the ontological foundations in which they are firmly grounded. For Christian Hesychasm these foundations can be seen in the idea of the ultimate difference between the divine "essence" (οὐσία) and divine "energy" (ἐνέργεια).

Actually, we are dealing here—though within a different framework of ideas—with the same problem of correlation (or transition) between the "One" and the "Many." While Western Christianity is, generally speaking, inclined to start with the notion of "essence" or "nature" (*esse*) of God, the Eastern Christian tradition prefers to begin with the concept of real "powers" or "potential creative abilities." As Henri de Regnon said at the end of the last century, "[T]he Greek [Christians] enter the tree of Porphyrius from below, starting from the concrete and actual individual, the way he exists in reality, with all the multitude of his essential or accidental properties."[18] In

---

templative technique which made use of the endless repetitions of the "divine names" was, in fact, quite close to the notion of the Muslim *dhikr* or chanting of God's name.

18. "Les grecs entrent dans l'arbre de Porphyre par en bas, par

other words, while Latin scholastic theology concentrated mainly on the concept of one essence and then descended down to the notion of active agents that embodied that essence, the Greek Orthodox Christianity took its initial stand with the concept of active agents that represent the Trinity, as well as with dynamic powers that are manifested by them, and only then was prepared to ascend towards the ultimate unity. For Eastern Orthodox Church an initial object of concrete experience and contemplation was always presented in the image of Trinity, while the indefinable and united divine essence was rather a matter of more abstract belief. The contemplative religious experience of Eastern Christianity, based on the notion of three distinctive hypostases of the Godhead, found itself a further expression in the concept of "energies" that emanate from God's essence and provide an intermediary ontological link between the higher God and the created universe.

The Hesychast doctrine, which found its fullest expression in the works of the fourteenth-century Byzantine scholar and theologian Gregory Palamas (1296-1359), was conceived as a bold attempt to bridge the gap between uncreated essence of God and created and finite nature of man. That also meant providing a possibility of approaching the essentially indefinable and incomprehensible Godhead while making use of our limited means of knowledge.

Hesychasts were, in fact, fully aware of the main premises of apophatic or "negative" theology suggested by Pseudo-Dionysius the Areopagite. Indeed, according to the apophatic tenets, the essence of God is absolutely indefinable; it cannot be grasped either by our senses or by the intellect, it is ever avoiding determination in human categories, ever evasive and ineffable. However, this Godhead, devoid of any qualities or attributes, reveals itself to us through its "energies," which are similar to the "energies" that remain inherent in ordinary

---

l'individu concret et subsistant, tel qu'il est dans la realité, avec tout l'ensemble de ses proprietés essentielles ou accidentielles."—H. de Regnon, *Études de théologie positive sur la sainte Trinité*, tome 1 (Paris, 1892), 278.

human beings. Even limited human "energy" or "potency" can be brought into some form of "communication" (κοινωνία or περιχωρήσις, literally, a "resonance," an "echo," a "harmony") with their divine counterparts.[19] In this "synergy," or "communion of energies," finite human nature can be purified through God's mercy, as well as owing to its own creative potentiality. In the words of Gregory Palamas, God can "deify" the created spirits, merging with them in their energies. It does not mean that God becomes united with the creatures in his "hypostasis," or in "person" (this union of "hypostases" exists only for Jesus Christ), and it does not mean that He becomes united with them in His divine essence (the ultimate difference between utterly ineffable, inconceivable essence of God and created, limited essence of man is something that stays forever, even after salvation), but in his mercy God allows for the possibility of a human participation in some of his divine energies.[20]

This concept of the "communion" or "concordance" (περιχωρήσις) of energies calls for the active and dynamic contribution of man, who should be prepared to act in harmony with the God's plan for the universe. In other words, while the union with the ineffable and inconceivable essence of God is absolutely impossible, there is a way of "participating" in this divine nature owing to the "communication" (κοινωνία) through energy,[21] and human beings should not forfeit the chance of this interplay.

---

19. In other words, if we interpret it in terms of Western Christianity: there cannot be any "analogy" between God and the rest of the universe, including man, and we cannot ever hope to construct a convincing *analogia entis* ("analogy of being"), but we can certainly opt for a tentative theological interpretation of the world, if we build it on the foundation of the "analogy of act," on the foundation of the same power or "energy" of love that unites us with God, as well as with one another.

20. Gregory Palamas, in *Parisinus Coislinianus*, 90 f. 145 V (unpublished manuscript). See J. Meiendorff, *A Study of Gregory Palamas* (London: Faith Press, 1962), 182.

21. The notion of this union was something which was presup-

It is important to understand that, according to the Hesychasts, God's energies are not the effects of His essence; they were not created in time, but are ever flowing out and beyond His nature. Even if creation had not taken place, the ever-emerging pattern of the energies would still be present. The energies are eternal, since God Himself is eternal; and the same kinds of energies (though less powerful and less bright) are ever shining forth in every created being. The whole of Hesychast theology can be summed up if we remember the ultimate definition suggested by Gregory Palamas: the energy is God Himself, but God is not His energy. The emanating energies reveal or express the "names" of God, though God cannot be completely defined by any of these attributes. In other words, the energy is a mirror, reflecting God, even though His essence remains invisible and devoid of form. The energies are the "rays of primordial light" (Pseudo-Dionysius), and they are ever working inside us through the Holy Spirit, because they are essentially the free gift of the Lord (and the very freedom of our own spirit is in itself a gift of the Lord; it is one of His own powers, which He brings forth to share with us). Through God's grace we receive the communication in energies—in fact, we receive everything but the identity of essence, since God's nature remains inconceivable and ineffable even after man's ultimate salvation.

---

posed in the apophatic and cataphatic theology of Pseudo-Dionysius. In the "Areopagites" we find the concept of two possible links between God and man. The first one is represented by the "unions" (ἑνώσεις); they are seldom revealed and only to the chosen ones. Pseudo-Dionysius calls them "secret houses" or "secret resting-places," it is a sort of secluded island (or a rare moment) inside mundane existence where God becomes attainable in contemplation. The second link, however, is freely given by God; it is built by the "processions" (πρόοδοι) of the Holy Spirit, by a series of its "manifestations" (ἐκφανσεῖς), as well as by the "powers" (δυνάμεις). Through the second link God Himself, in His energies, descends towards man. And, in the opinion of Pseudo-Dionysius, the "names" of God (that is, His different attributes presented in Scripture) are revealed in accordance with His various energies.

Taking into account this concept of the divine energy, we can examine the Eastern Orthodox experience of the triadic Godhead. In Western Christianity, as we mentioned, the emphasis is laid on the unity of essence, so that three hypostases are regarded rather like three possible relations, existing between the aspects of this essence. According to the Eastern Christian dogmatics, we cannot know "what" God is, we only know that He "is," since in the history of salvation He revealed Himself in three concrete hypostases: as the Father, the Son, and the Holy Spirit. The triadic unity cannot be logically derived out of the concept of the essence; it cannot be proved or demonstrated. It only exists as a primary direct experience: there is one essence, or nature (οὐσία) which remains ever invisible, but three "faces" (πρόσωπα),[22] that can be experienced in energies. In the words of a Byzantine theologian, Gregory of Nazianzus, "when I speak about God, you should simultaneously become aware of one flash of light and of the three flashes. Three in qualities, hypostases, or persons, if you prefer to call it thus (since we would not quibble about names, [and will agree] that all these syllables convey the same meaning); but one in its "essence" or Godhead."[23] The concept of these hypostases becomes clearer if we consider that, according to Byzantine scholars, the same energy begins in the Father, passes through the Son, and finds its completion in the Holy Spirit—so that ultimately there is one action, one effort (and

22. The very Greek term πρόσωπον ("person," "face") is rarely used in the Western tradition, since it can also mean a "mask," an "appearance," something utterly misleading and artificial (it was used, for instance, to refer to a mask or artificial image, used in theatre performances). The Eastern Christianity to some extent retained the dangerous complexity of the various meanings contained in this, when it deliberately opted for ther term "hypostasis" rather than the Western "person." The connotation is probably unavoidable when speaking about the three "faces," or three "manifestations" of God. Even the Western Christian tradition does, to some extent, retain this ambiguity, since Latin "persona" can still mean a "mask" or "cover" that disguises the real face.

23. Gregory of Nazianzus, *Oratio*, 39.11

not three different actions). The concept of energy reflects the united and synchronized life, the dynamic communion of the three persons: the hypostases are not intermingled, they are not merged together, but they are ever united through the energy of love.

And that basic relationship ultimately sets a pattern for all human beings. Since ἐνέργεια is not just an aspect of the essence, nor is it a symbol of the ineffable nature, but a dynamic flow which comes from God, it both safeguards the inconceivable character of this essence and creates a channel of communication between God and man. In the words of Gregory Palamas, we can approach God "because for God there is the 'essence,' and there is something else, which is not an essence but could not be called an accidental quality; namely, He has will and energy."[24] While remaining totally transcendent and unattainable, God, nevertheless, totally offers Himself forth in His energy. Being identical with energy and wholly present in it, He reveals Himself as a living, actively participating entity. Various divine energies do not signify the splitting up of the divine essence, they do not represent different levels of embodiment and condensing of the divine light—their only meaning and goal is to convey the living and active nature of the Godhead itself.

The act of creation is ever separated from the free flow of eternal energies. Creation means a sudden breach in time, a sudden appearence of objects and beings *ex nihilo*,[25] while the energy can only be present as a constantly renewing pattern of interrelations, of mutual strivings and yearnings. For Christian Neoplatonic scholars (as well as for the Kashmir Śaivites), the

---

24. "ἔχει ἄρα ὁ θεὸς καὶ ὅ οὐσία, καὶ ὅ μη οὐσία, κἄν εἰ μὴ συμβεβηκὸς καλοῖτο, τὴν θείαν δηλονότι βουλὴν καὶ ἐνέργειαν."—Gregory Palamas, *Capita physica, theologica. Patristica graeca*, tome CL, col. 1216d.

25. As Gregory of Nyssa put it: Why should we wish to feel ourselves a "microcosm" that reflects the whole of the universe, if the energy which sets us apart from the rest of the creation is a far more precious and subtle divine gift?

emanation of the divine light was bound to become more and more dense, transforming on its way into the rigid shapes of the created universe, but the Hesychast ἐνέπγεια never assumes the rigid and frozen outlines of inanimate objects. It can exist essentially only in the form of a living pattern, never seeking to find itself a definitive shape or body. The energy, in terms of Byzantine theologians, is the "light of Mount Tabor," the light of the divine "epiphany" (ἐπιφάνεια), a self-revealing light, totally devoid of any material substrate.[26]

Now, we should not be surprised by the new turn these Hesychast ideas took in the later history of the Eastern Orthodox Church. In fact, if we are prepared to concede that the living pulsation of divine energies has something in common with the *spanda* or *sphoṭa* vibration of early Vedānta, it seems only natural that the next step was to equate this energy of love with the energy inherent in Speech, that is, with its power to "call," or "to give names."

By the end of the nineteenth century, Hesychast theology had undergone a veritable revival among Russian religious philosophers. Although for several centuries it was regarded as something verging on heresy and deemed unacceptable for the official Orthodox Church, it nevertheless proved to be potent and attractive enough to win over many prominent religious thinkers. In his work *Essays on Ancient Symbolism and Mythology*, Alexei Losev, who was quite enchanted by Hesychast teaching, said:

> The Palamites taught that the light of Tabor, as seen by the disciples of Christ and his followers, was neither the

26. Actually this mysterious "Light of Tabor" functionally assumes in Eastern Christianity the role of "recognition" (*pratyabhijñā*) or sudden illumination (*pratibhā*). The "tongues of flame," traditionally associated with the miracle of Pentecost and the light from the Mount Tabor, represent the living reminder, so that the apostles (as well as the rest of the mankind) would realize in a sudden "flashing up" the significance of the coming of Christ. The energy of the Tabor Light carries on the living communion of every human being with the Holy Spirit.

> essence of God (since the energy can be communicated, while the essence of God is incommunicable) nor created nature (since otherwise creatures could be deified through their own nature), but an eternal energy of the God's essence, different from the essence but inseparable from it. This energy . . . while communicating itself to the creature and deifying it . . . does not itself become this creature but continues to be inseparable from God—hence, it continues to be God Himself. The very name "God," they said, should be applied not only to God's essence, but also to His energies. Every energy and all energies together are God Himself, although God is not an energy—neither one of them nor all of them put together.[27]

According to this tradition, language itself, or "speech" capable of "giving names," is regarded as an energy emanation of the primordial divine essence (*esse*, οὐσία).

Losev was a thinker who gravitated towards Hesychast theology. He could not really pursue this interest, however, since the time itself was far from favorable to such theoretical exercises. In fact, he only wrote one book on similar metaphysical problems (before winding up in a prison camp), and that does not even mention God or God's nature. It deals exclusively with the "energy of the name."[28] However, even before his time, the philosophical interest in the inherent potencies of language was quite prominent in Russian religious philosophy. It was directly related to the ancient Orthodox tradition called *imyaslaviye*, or the "glorification of the name," and one of its propounders, Father Pavel Florensky, traced main tenets of this teaching not only to its origin within the fold of the Hesychast Byzantine sect, but also to some contemporary

---

27. See A. F. Losev, *Ocherki antichnogo simvolizma i mifologii* (Moscow, 1930), 84.

28. A. F. Losev, *Filosofiya imeni* (Moscow, 1927; reprinted by Moscow State University Press in 1990).

philological and linguistic ideas of Alexandre Potebnia.[29]

The "name" (*imya*), that is, any "real," "true," "correct" word, is the only possible concrete manifestation of pure being or pure consciousness. It is much more closely related to the energy of that being than any of the objects it might be applied to. The "name" still radiates from inside with the energy of the divine presence; moreover, the "name" is actually this energy constantly at work in our world, as well as the only means of direct communication with God. When Adam was giving names to the objects and beings of the newly created world, he was not (and could not) invent them out of nowhere; the names were already present, they existed before the moment of creation as an energy pattern that continues to speak forth before the appearance of the first speaker.

Indeed, only "names" (or "words") are capable of accomplishing two theological aspirations simultaneously: they can create a distant possibility of apophatic approach to God and provide human beings with the means of cataphatic revelation.

According to the apophatic (or "negative") theology, the essence of God is ever concealed, it is ineffable and inconceivable. In Indian terms, we can say that it is essentially *nirguṇa*—devoid of qualities or attributes. Whatever the theological implications, pure *ātman* can never be pinpointed by logical argumentation or seized by sense experience, since it is the very foundation of every cognition and perception; the self cannot turn around to grasp its own essence, cannot become its

---

29. Incidentally, in his major work, entitled "Mysl i yazyk" ("Thought and Language") and published in 1862, Potebnia brings his philosophy of language into a close contact with the concept of art. He maintains, for example, that art, "just like the word itself, is not so much the outward expression, as the means of creating the idea; its aim, just like the aim of the word, is to produce a certain subjective transformation both inside [the soul] of the artist and inside [the soul] of the understanding recepient; art, too, is not an ἔργον ("accomplished work") but an ἐνέργεια ("energy")—something that ever goes on being created."—Alexandre Potebnia, "Thought and Language," in A. Potebnia, *Estetika i poetika* ("Aesthetics and Poetics") (Moscow, 1976), 183.

own object. However, according to the Advaita point of view, there is a way of staying in intimate closeness to *ātman*, even though one can never hope to penetrate its inner being. And this way is suggested by language itself. In fact, within the very sphere of language, there are known to exist indirect means of communication that help us to stay close to this ineffable entity. The most powerful of these words are the sayings of revelation, not invented by any human mind. Be it the words of the Veda or the parables of the New Testament, or even some basic texts of Kashmir Śaivism—they all abound with metaphors and word-play, poetical embellishments and riddles, which seem to be superfluous and irritating in a philosophical text, but are, in fact, indispensable when talking about pure being or pure consciousness.[30] Even when ordinary human beings use metaphors, symbols, or allegories, or when poets or philosophers use the deceptive, inventive, glittering tricks of poetical language, they—perhaps, without even being aware of it—actually strive to dwell in the radiant vicinity of pure *ātman* (or God's οὐσία), since the *ātman*, being totally invisible, can be traced only through its luminous halo of energies. Words, especially poetical words, survive in this rarefied atmosphere where logic would not be able to breathe—they survive and accomplish their task precisely because they share the same energy that is ever emanating from this inconceivable and immeasurable "black hole."

Now, when we examine cataphatic (or "positive") theol-

---

30. Hence the Buddhist idea of *ṣaṇḍabhāṣā* or "dark," "twilight" language, which is supposed to be full of special significance precisely because it is so dark. One could also remember Abhinavagupta's idea of *japa* as this special, "inaudible" language, in which God speaks to himself when he does not want to be overheard. And, of course, the repressed energy of mantras is by no means diminished by the fact that they cannot be interpreted or translated literally; what matters is the power within them, which is still intact. The power of the sacred syllable *Oṃ* or *praṇava* is derived straight from the verb root *pra-ṇu*: "to sound," "to echo," "to reverberate," but at the same time it acquires additional force from the basic root *nu*—"to command," "to summon," or "to praise."

ogy, it is important to remember that its very possibility is based on God's own merciful decision to descend to the creatures, by stepping down the ladder of "theophanies." God is manifested in the created universe, but He manifests Himself far more fully in His energies. Thomas Aquinas would have said that the possibility of knowing God is mainly based on the "analogy of being" (*analogia entis*), because God Himself is ever setting up a pattern, a model for the created universe to follow. Meanwhile, for Christian Hesychasts (as well as for early Vedāntins, still oscillating between the ideas of *nirguṇa* and *saguṇa Brahman*), God can only be known through His energies, which provide a vibrant, pulsating pattern, and which animate finite creatures giving them the gift of life.

In terms of cataphatic theology, both the universe and finite human beings were created *ex nihilo* by a special effort of God's will; they do not emanate from Him as in Neoplatonic or Kashmir Śaivite cosmogony. They do not represent a mere condensation or obfuscation of the divine light, but rather an interruption, a qualitative "leap" or "break" within a continuity.

We cannot say whether creation itself was "real" or "unreal," and since all human beings were also created, we cannot say whether human essence is real or not; the only thing that is clear and definite is that the energies are real. Moreover, man himself is no less inconceivable and ungraspable in his essence, for he was created "in the likeness" (ὅμοούσιος) of God. Man's "nature" or "being" (οὐσία) is different from God's, but still remains as dark and ineffable a mystery. You cannot hope to "know" God, just as you cannot hope to "know" your own being (in Indian terms we would have said that all *ātmans* are essentially *nirguṇa*), but the task and purpose of the created world is not to contemplate God's essence, but to participate[31] in his energies. The free movement of man towards

---

31. This theory of active "participation" of man in God's "energies" (or in the energy of the language) has found itself a curious development in some aspects of Gadamer's hermeneutical concept of *Zugehörigkeit* ("belonging to," hence "participation in") as fundamental notion which only later comes to be split into the duality of the

God is simultaneously presented as an equally free gift or mercy of divine "energy" (ἐνέργεια). There is no gap between human freedom and divine mercy, since the latter is always working from within, revealing itself above all in human creative potency.

According to the theological concept originating in the teaching of Byzantine Hesychasts, one can actually participate in God's initial plan for the universe only if one is prepared to use the same powers, the same energies. And the most potent of these powers is the power of speech, the power to evoke new meanings and create, along with God, through a surge of vibrating and alive aesthetical effort. The relationship here is the one found in modern theories of art, where the artist and the spectator are considered to be essentially equal in their creative activity, and where the ability to create is regarded as essentially identical to the ability to receive, to grasp the elusive aesthetic meaning.[32] The spectator is no longer a pliant and passive receptacle for some idea or image; he or she participates in the birth of that meaning. Two creative spirits are working on it together, in unison (we might even say: in περιχωρήσις); and the common ground, where they can meet each other, is supplied by speech, by poetical language.[33] So, from the point of view of both Hesychast theology and early

---

subject and the object. Owing to that "participation" in the language realities we can say that it is not our task to create new meanings—rather, it is the meaning itself that utlimately guides and directs us.

32. Somewhat later on we are going to deal with a similar concept of *sahṛdaya* or the "same-hearted" listener, developed in Abhinavagupta's aesthetical theory.

33. In order to communicate, God and the finite creature (or artist and spectator) are in need of a common ground: and what they need, first and foremost, is an analogy which assumes the form of creative, artistic effort—or at least, an art object (and language is certainly a main art object, created by God as the ultimate artist, since it is a direct manifestation of His creative energy) through which they can relate to each other. Only thus they can enter into communion, attain mutual participation. In one of his works dealing with drama

Vedānta, the main duty of an adept is his willing agreement, his conscious effort to participate in the divine energies. Only by acknowledging this participation, only by exposing himself to the calling and invocation of that ἐνέργεια, ever present in the divine Speech, can man hope to build up a relationship with God. But as soon as this relationship is established, Speech reveals its inner pattern as a threefold pulsation of "I," "thou," "it" (or "him/her"), with the higher level of inconceivable οὐσία (or *nirguṇa-brahma*, that is, "pure consciousness") providing a silent foundation as an ever-present fourth element of the structure.[34] In this way, the concept of Speech as divine energy (ἐνέργεια) capable of generating meanings brings us close to the understanding of the nature of art.

J.-P. Sartre writes: "L'acte imageant, pris dans sa generalité, est celui d'une conscience qui vise un objet absent ou inexistant à travers une certaine réalité que j'ai nommé ailleurs *analogon* et qui fonctionne non comme un signe mais comme un symbole"—"The act of imagination taken in its generality is the act of consciousness which aims at an absent or nonexistent object through a certain reality that I defined elsewhere an *analogon* ("analogy"); this reality functions not as a sign but as a symbol." See J.-P. Sartre, "L'acteur," in J.-P. Sartre, *Un théâtre de situations* (Paris: Gallimard, 1973), 199.

34. One recalls that L. Renou, when he was discussing the nature of a Tāntric mantra in contrast to that of a Vedic one, said in one of his works: "It tends to stay beyond language, eventually even up to the very sphere of silence"—"Il tend à se situer au-delà du langage, éventuellement jusqu'à la zone même du silence." L. Renou, "Le destin du Veda dans l'Inde," in L. Renou, *Études Védiques et Pāṇinéennes*, t. 6, pp. 11-12.

12 Abhinavagupta's Aesthetics

If a correspondence exists between the essentially dynamic approach of early Vedānta and the tenets of Kashmir Śaivism, it will probably be found mostly within the frame of Abhinavagupta's aesthetical theory. This is only natural because the only possible way to harmonize or "synchronize" energies is to bring them into resonance in a mutual creative effort (preferably in the field where you are free to play with words and meanings). Of course, the concept of an instant illumination (*pratibhā*), which was so important in Bhartṛhari's system, found a close counterpart in the theory of "recognition" or *pratyabhijñā*. However, regarding the echoing vibration that suddenly unites God and man in the same word energy, there seems to be even more striking parallel in Abhinavagupta's idea of aesthetic pleasure understood as ontological passion.

Though directly influenced by Kashmir Śaivism and grammarians like Bhartṛhari, Abhinavagupta was also greatly indebted to the aesthetical theory of his time. It is usually assumed that he came to aesthetical and literary criticism rather late in life, after his own philosophical concepts had taken shape. His most famous works on this subject are, indoubtedly, *Locana* ("The Eye"), the commentary on the celebrated *Dhvanyāloka* ("The Light of Dhvani") by Ānandavardhana, and an extensive commentary on *Naṭya-śāstra* ("The Treatise on Drama Acting"). Of course, any detailed analysis of Abhinavagupta's aesthetical categories largely falls beyond the scope of the present book, and in any case there are dozens of works dealing with the subject.[35] I wish, though, to draw atten-

35. A detailed bibliography as well as the list of the most impor-

tion to some allusions in these works to the concept of a higher Speech. As Abhinavagupta puts it in his comentary on *Naṭya-śāstra*, "the poet is like Prajāpati, from whose desire the world is born, since he is endowed with a power (*śakti*) to give birth to wonderful and previously unknown things; this [power] is bestowed [upon him] by the divine higher speech (*parā-vāg*), otherwise called *pratibhā*, which has its abode in his own heart and is perpetually scintillating (*udita*) [there]."[36]

So let us turn, then, to Abhinavagupta's ideas on the aesthetical problems related to language, and to his concept of the powers of speech and its ability to convey meaning. We will try to determine what, according to Abhinavagupta, is being revealed in a poetical text, what are the specific ways and means of this revealing, what is being received by the listener, and how it is harmonized with the non-dualist Śaivite concept of the universe.

Beginning with Abhinavagupta's predecessor Ānandavardhana (ninth century), Indian aesthetics became interested in the evocative function of language. In other words, theoreticians of literature, besides dealing with specific technical problems of poetics, recognized the ability of language to convey or imply certain meanings without expressing them explicitly. By that time there already existed an elaborated classification of metaphors, poetical embellishments, and embroideries, but the latter were largely regarded as technical devices, as specific skills demanded of a poet, as something that could be developed and perfected, something that could be both

---

tant Sanskrit works on poetics can be found in: *The "Dhvanyāloka" of Ānandavardhana, with the "Locana" of Abhinavagupta*, translated by D. H. H. Ingalls, J. M. Masson, and M. V. Patwardhan, edited with an introduction by D. H. H. Ingalls (Cambridge, Mass.: Harvard University Press, 1990).

36. "kaver api svahṛdayāyatanasatatoditapratibhābhidhānaparāvāgdevatānugrahotthitavicitrāpūrvārthanirmāṇaśaktiśālinaḥ prajāpater iva kāmajanitajagataḥ /"—*Naṭyaśāstra with the Abhinavabhāratī of Abhinavagupta*, ed. Ramakrishna Kavi, Gaekwad's Oriental Series, XXXVI, Vol. I, 1-7 (Baroda, 1956), 4.

taught and mastered.[37] Ānandavardhana became one of the founders of the so-called "school of *dhvani*" or "suggested meaning"; he was the first theoretician of literature to maintain that language had at its disposal the power of indirect communication (*vyañjana-vyāpāra*), inherent not only in poetical texts but—to a varying extent—in every utterance and saying.[38]

Propounding the theory of *dhvani*, both Ānandavardhana and his follower Abhinavagupta relate it to the teaching of the grammarians, in particular, to that of Bhartṛhari. Of course, from the point of view of terminology, Bhartṛhari's *dhvani* ("ideal sound"), which is essentially but one of the means of self-manifestation of *sphoṭa*, has little in common with the concept of *dhvani* as "suggested meaning." Nevertheless, the spirit of Bhartṛhari's teaching comes very close to the tenets of Kashmirian aestheticians. In the words of Ānandavardhana,

> the first among the wise ones are the grammarians (*vaiyākaraṇa*), since grammar is the root of all knowledge; and they used the [word] *dhvani* [to define] articulated [ideal] syllables. So it is maintained that other scholars, following them and capable of discerning the essence

---

37. The theories of metaphors (*rūpaka*) and the figures of speech were mainly propounded by Bhāmaha and Daṇḍin (around eighth century).

38. Coming back to the teaching of Bhartṛhari, one can recall the technical term that is used twice in the first chapter of his *Vākya-padīya*. It is the word *vyaṅgya* that emerges in the 93rd *kārikā* of "Brahma-kaṇḍa" (possibly, with reference to Patañjali's theory), and the terms *vyaṅgya* and *vyañjaka* that appear in the 97th *kārikā*. *Vyaṅgya* simply means something that is "signified" or "manifested" by language, while *vyañjaka* corresponds to *vācaka* or *saṃjñā*, that is, to the words as the means or instruments of this "manifestation." There is still no hint of possible developments that were later to become so prominent in Ānandavardhana's "theory of suggestion." Yet, in its own way, Bhartṛhari's choice of words was, perhaps, rather peculiar and unusual.

of poetry, [define] the unity of the signifier and the signified (*vācya-vācaka-saṃmiśra*), or the essence of the word, as poetry, giving it the name of *dhvani* owing to the same ability to convey suggested meaning (*vyañjakatva*).
(*Dhvanyāloka*, 1.13).[39]

And Abhinavagupta, in his turn, emphasizes in his commentary *Locana* (1.4) that he has no serious differences with the followers of the theory of *sphoṭa*.

Before trying to understand Abhinavagupta's concept of *dhvani*, let us consider some basic terms of Sanskrit poetics.

When we are dealing with the literal sense of the utterance, the words that convey it are called *abhidhā* (or *vācaka*), the literal meaning is *abhidheya* (*vācya*), while the process, the action, the phenomenon itself is *abhidhāna* (*vacana*). Most often in this case we have simple denotation: the word or the saying directly points or refers to some specific object.

Of course, literary critics and theoreticians were perceptive enough to acknowledge that poetry makes use of other meanings of the word, directly excluding the possibility of literal interpretation. Ānandavardhana's predecessor, Bhāmaha, and his contemporary, Rudraṭa, analyzed the origin and rules of functioning of the so-called "figurative meaning" (*lakṣaṇa*); the word or the saying conveying it is usually called *lakṣaṇika*, while the meaning itself bears the name *lakṣya*. *Lakṣaṇa* is mainly concerned about creating metaphors (*rūpaka*), language embellishments (*alaṅkāra*), instances of ambiguous, figurative sense (*vakrokti*).

Ānandavardhana was the first aesthetician to maintain that every saying was also endowed with a certain evocative power, a power to generate suggested meanings. New fields of meaning

---

39. Ānandavardhana, *Dhvanyāloka*, 1.13: "prathame hi vidvāṃso vaiyākaraṇaḥ vyākaraṇamūlatvāt sarvavidyānām / te ca śrūyamāṇeṣu varṇeṣu dhvanir iti vyavaharanti / tathaivānyais tanmatānusāribhiḥ sūribhiḥ kāvyatattvārthadarśibhir vācyavācakasaṃmiśraḥ śabdātmā kāvyam iti vyapadeśyo vyañjakatvasāmyād dhvanir ity uktaḥ /

are born not by broadening or stretching the initial sense (whether literal or figurative), but through the working of a totally different power, inherent in the word itself, as well as in specific and unusual combinations of the words used by the poet. Sometimes relentlessly twisting the laws of logic, sometimes daring to use a manifestly unsuitable word, the poet reaches out for new and unexpected senses, for something that cannot be explained or motivated. Poetical meaning achieved in this way could never be expressed in other words, and the text itself could never be paraphrased or changed without impairing this elusive suggestion. The subtle core of meaning lacks any "material" substrate, it is only hinted at; we can merely guess what the author was trying to convey, without ever coming close enough to its precise definition or grasping. To some extent "suggestion" remains a mystery, a riddle even for the poet himself. The power of suggested meaning (*vyañjana-vyāpāra*) is generated by the language itself, the poet is only the suitable medium or instrument to channel it out to the audience. If "suggestion" is a melody, then the poet is not a composer but rather a flute to play it on. And it was this suggestive energy of poetical language that came to be known as *dhvani* (see *Dhvanyāloka*, 1.2, etc.). The saying or the word that conveys this meaning is called *vyañjaka*, while the meaning itself is usually termed *vyaṅgya*.

In contrast to the metaphorical or figurative meaning (*lakṣaṇa*), *dhvani* does not exist as an opposition, a challenge to the literal sense. Both *abhidhā* and *lakṣaṇa* are still present, they are not cancelled by the working of *dhvani*, since they cannot hinder its power, cannot prevent *dhvani* from being expressed. "Suggested meaning" reaches out through them; it is capable of using anything as its means of conveyance. Both *abhidhā* and *lakṣaṇa* are subordinated and conquered by *dhvani* when it moves on, being carried away by its passionate longing to reveal something about the universe that only language can know. As it is said in Abhinavagupta's *Locana* (1.13), "*dhvani* is indeed the basic sphere of suggestion."[40]

---

40. Abhinavagupta, *Locana*, 1.13: "vyaṅgyapradhānye hi dhvaniḥ."

Of course, it is often rather difficult to pinpoint the meaning of a particular term of Sanskrit poetics, especially when one is dealing with such an intentionally vague and ambiguous word as *dhvani*. In Western critical literature *vyañjana* and *dhvani* are sometimes rendered as "suggestion," the "implied," "figurative" meaning, even the "symbolical" meaning of an utterance or a single word. However, that varied list of synonyms often tends to be quite misleading, since owing to it *dhvani* becomes easily confused and lumped together with "metaphor," "allegory," "symbol," and other similar terms of Western poetics.[41]

After all, what is the crucial difference between a "figurative" (*lakṣaṇa*) and a "suggested" (*vyañjana*) meaning, how can they be distinguished?

I would say that it can be explained with the help of a very simple simile. Then *abhidhā* or "literal" meaning can be likened to a concise inventory, a brief summary scribbled on the top of the envelope; one need not open the envelope, since the summary of the contents gives a definite enough and true enough picture of the contents. So, *lakṣaṇa*, or "figurative," "secondary" meaning, represents the beautiful stamps, vignettes, and embroideries on the envelope; they can be easily

---

41. Generally speaking, Western aesthetics does not really distinguish between "figurative" and "suggested" meaning. However, certain indications that help to separate them can be found in Paul Ricoeur's notion of *la métaphore vive* ("living metaphor") and *la métaphore morte* ("dead metaphor"), where the former roughly corresponds to Abhinavagupta's *dhvani* as a means of revealing new, as yet unsuspected meanings. Describing the functioning of a "living metaphor," Ricoeur says: "C'est cette véhémence ontologique qui détache la signification de son propre ancrage, la libère comme forme d'un mouvement et la transporte dans un champ nouveau, qu'elle peut informer de sa propre vertu figurative" ("It is this ontological striving which tears signification away from its own anchorage, liberates it, setting it as a form of movement, and finally brings it into a new field, that is capable of letting it know its own figurative power"). Paul Ricoeur, *La métaphore vive* (Paris: Editions du Seuil, 1975), 379.

replaced by other similar embellishments in accordance with the tastes and preferences of this or that addressee. *Vyañjana* or *dhvani* ("suggested" meaning) is nothing but the letter itself, the letter which can only be read if an addressee is bright enough to realize the impeding necessity of ripping open the envelope. And, incidentally, in that moment it becomes quite clear that the envelope itself was used merely for the purpose of safekeeping and delivering the letter.

However, the simile does not end there. The letter which reaches its destination was initially posted in order to convey a certain message. To my mind (if, of course, I am not mistaken in my interpretations of the basic notions of Śaivite aesthetical theories), the message itself is represented by *rasa*.[42] The Sanskrit term *rasa* is one of those ambiguous words that are extremely difficult to translate; it is usually rendered as "taste," "flavour," or even "poetical imagination," "poetical intuition," "powerful emotion," "aesthetical pleasure."[43] Again, the words themselves do not explain anything, they remain empty and

---

42. There is again, curiously enough, quite a significant appearance of this term in Bhartṛhari's treatise. He says quite explicitly:

Having split into perfect forms,
    Speech is the higher "taste" (*rasa*);
[So,] just like the light
    of the higher merit,
    [grammar] shows the way to it.

Prāptarūpavibhāgāyā yo vācaḥ paramo rasaḥ /
Yat tat puṇyatamaṃ jyotis tasya mārgo 'yam āñjasaḥ //
(*Vākya-padīya*, 1.12)

Even though Bhartṛhari was clearly not concerned about any concept of *rasa*, the choice of words remains quite suggestive.

43. For example, S. J. Anand Amaladass in his analysis of *dhvani* and *rasa* in Abhinavagupta's aesthetics keeps coming back to the well-known simile of the "body" and the "soul," saying that *dhvani*, being the "soul" of poetical text, can only function through bodily manifestations, that is, through emotions, passions (*rasa*), in order to generate emotional response in the soul of listener.—S. J. Anand Amaladass, *Philosophical Implications of Dhvani: Experience*

hollow shells if one is not trying to grasp the image that lays behind them, the function they are supposed to play in the general structure.

Before Ānandavardhana and Abhinavagupta, the theory of *rasa* was already extensively discussed by aestheticians and literary critics. One of the reknown authorities on the subject was Bharata (c. sixth century), the celebrated author of *Naṭya-śāstra* ("The Śāstra on Dramatic Art"); for him *rasa* was directly correlated to a "persistent mood," "powerful emotion" (*sthāyibhāva*), or, at least, was considered to be generated by this emotion.[44] Ānandavardhana's contemporary, Bhaṭṭanāyaka (ninth century) equated *rasa* with "enjoyment" or "pleasure" (*bhoga*), deriving the whole concept from the Mīmāṃsā theory of the inner "efficacy," "potency" of the word (*śabda-bhāvanā*).

According to Ānandavardhana and Abhinavagupta, *rasa* cannot be reduced to mere "tasting," "enjoyment," even if what is implied here presents a specific form of "aesthetic enjoyment." In other words, *rasa* should include not only (or not so much) the element of emotional response, but also the element of conscious perception, the element of "knowledge." And besides that, there is an important function that only *rasa* can perform, something that brings it close enough to the notion of

---

of Symbol Language in Indian Aesthetics (Vienna, 1984), 130-39. I find it rather hard to accept this kind of interpretation, and for me the difficulty starts with the rendering of *ātman* as "soul." Incidentally, the scholar himself became aware of certain stumbling blocks inherent in this interpretation: having translated *dhvani* as "symbol," he then tried to apply to it the hermeneutical approach of Paul Ricoeur—only to discover later with some bewilderment that for Ricoeur *le symbole* is totally devoid of any emotional content.

44. In Bharata's *Naṭya-śāstra* (6.15), we get a list of eight main types of *rasa*. It includes "erotic" (*śṛṅgāra*), "comic" (*hāsya*), "compassionate" (*karuṇa*), "fierce" (*raudra*), "manly" (*vīra*), "fearsome" (*bhayānaka*), "loathsome" (*bībhatsa*) and "surprising" (*adbhuta*) ones. Even Bharata himself distinguished between a *rasa* and a "persistent emotion" (*sthāyibhāva*) without, however, specifying the nature of this distinction. Different *stāyibhāvas* are enumerated in *Naṭya-śāstra*, 6.17.

κάθαρσις the way it was developed in Plato's *Phaedo* (where "knowledge" is likened to purification rites) and Aristotle's *Poetics* (chapter 6, where it is dealt with in connection with the theory of drama).

Returning to our analogy, we can say that as soon as the letter is really received and read by an addressee, the message is already conveyed. And the important thing about this message (*rasa*) is the fact that if it ever comes to be perceived, it is grasped suddenly, in a flash (*sphuṭatva*). Actually we are dealing here with a concept that was known to us under a different name: the idea of *rasa* in Abhinavagupta's aesthetics to some extent refers us back to Bhartṛhari's *pratibhā* and Abhinavagupta's own *pratyabhijñā*. *Rasa* flashes out suddenly, and, in the words of *Dhvanyāloka*, "it can never be an object of direct word definition" (*Dhvanyāloka*, 1.4).[45]

Rasa in Abhinavagupta's theory can hardly be interpreted as persistent, powerful, or even exceptionally pure emotion. From the context of both *Dhvanyāloka* and *Locana* it is quite clear that "emotion" or "mood" (*sthāyibhāva*) is rather to be regarded as a locus or accidental manifestation of *rasa*; *rasa* is accompanied and recognized by the distinctive mark of "enjoyment" but cannot be on any account simply reduced to it. As Abhinavagupta puts it,

> [aesthetical] enjoyment (*bhoga*) is produced not only by poetic words but rather by the removal of obstacles coming from the blinding darkness generated by confused ignorance (*moha*). In over-worldly enjoyment which comes in this way and is otherwise named "sweetness" (*asvāda*) . . . the principal meaning would be the "suggested" (*dhvanana*) one. As soon as this suggested meaning is implied, *rasa* is assumed to be capable of generating enjoyment. Since "enjoyment" (*bhoga*) is nothing else but the wondrous vibration of pleasure (*camatkāra*) which originates in aesthetical passion (*rasyamānata*). . . . We

---

45. Ānandavardhana, *Dhvanyāloka*, 1.4: "na tu sākṣāc chabdavyāpāraviṣaya iti /"

> agree that aesthetical enjoyment is akin to the joy of [recognizing oneself as] the higher Brahman (*Locana*, 2.4).[46]

And somewhat later in the text Abhinavagupta emphasizes again that *rasas* are conveyed only through "suggestion" (*abhivyañjyante*).

So, the letter safely reached its destination, the message was received. Its delivery is acknowledged by the addressee in a sudden "flash" of enlightenment (*pratibhā*), and, what is much more important, it is immediately "recognized" as a meaningful message. The recognition itself becomes possible only because—even before the instance of delivery—the addressee had already possessed a similar knowledge without being aware of it. In this moment of aesthetic passion the listener, the addressee, becomes equally great with the poet (or the poetical text) who is addressing him.

We now approach another aesthetical concept which was very prominent both in Ānandavardhana's treatise and in Abhinavagupta's commentary. It is the notion of *sahṛdaya* (lit. "the same-hearted one") or the "discerning listener." In Western critical literature the term is usually rendered as "understanding," "sensitive" reader, someone who is himself skilful in poetical games, a person of "refined taste" (D. H. H. Ingalls in his translation of *Dhvanyāloka* defines him as a "connoisseur"). To my mind, however, in Abhinavagupta's theory the bond existing between the poet and the listener could hardly be explained either by their emotional contact or even by the degree of cultural refinement of the respective audience.

According to the notions of Abhinavagupta's *Locana*, both cultural refinement and technical skills (*vyutpatti*) of the

46. Abhinavagupta, *Locana*, 2.4: "bhogo 'pi kāvyaśabdena kriyate api tu ghanamohāndyasaṅkaṭatānivṛttidvareṇa asvādāparanāmni . . . bhoge kartavye lokottare dhvananavyāpāra eva mūrdhābhiṣiktaḥ / tac cedaṃ bhogakṛttvaṃ rasasya dhvananīyatve siddhe daivasiddham / rasyamānatoditacamatkārān atiriktatvād bhogasyeti / . . . parabrahmāsvādasabrahmacāritvaṃ cāstv asya rasāsvādasya /"

poet and the listener come useful only as long as they deal with external embellishments (*alaṅkāra*) of the poetical text. We can diligently invent or cleverly discern metaphors, allegories, and other means of "figurative" meaning (*lakṣaṇa*), but all these culturally polished methods fall short of their goal as soon as we turn to the meaning which is only "suggested" (*vyañjana*, *dhvani*). In a short verse from *Locana* Abhinavagupta says:

> The cow of Speech
> is being milked for this *rasa*
> for the sake of her thirsty little ones;
> And it can hardly be compared
> with something that is being
> [dilgently] milked by the scholars.[47]
> (*Locana*, 1.6)

The "little ones" (*bāla*) belonging to the sacred cow of Speech are both the poets (*kavi*) and the "same-hearted" listeners (*sahṛdaya*)—in fact, those who allow Speech to work through them, to pulsate and reach out through the means of the poetical text. The communion between the poet and the listener is taking place on the ontological level; what is being revealed and "recognized" in the moment of poetical passion (*rasa*) is language itself, which existed long before the text was being uttered or heard. Even *camatkāra*, or the vibrating joy which accompanies aesthetical pleasure, is essentially not an emotional reaction but rather a moment of epiphany, the joyful amazement which comes with the successful solution of a complicated word-riddle.

Taken from this perspective, poetry and literature (as well as, for this matter, dramatic art) are never regarded by Abhinavagupta as mere "entertainment" (*vinoda*) or "pleasure" (*prīti*); they are usually correlated with the manifestation of

47. Abhinavagupta, *Locana*, 1.6:

Vāgdhenur dugdha etaṃ hi rasaṃ yadbālatṛṣṇyā /
Tena nāsya samaḥ sa syād duhyate yogibhir hi yaḥ //

bliss (*ānanda*) coming from the knowledge of Brahman.[48] In other words, Abhinavagupta's theory of aesthetics has a pronounced ontological and theological flavour: *dhvani* as suggested meaning is radically different from any mastered technical and cultural accomplishments (*vyutpatti*), while *rasa* as passion of recognition is radically different from the easily manipulated and constructed emotional states. In one of the passages of Ānandavardhana's *Dhvanyāloka* (1.6), we find a memorable image of the goddess Sarasvatī who, working through great poets, "pours out this entity (*arthavastu*) which is similar to the radiance and is being defined as a sudden intermittent flash of light."[49] The "entity" implied here is *rasa*; it is placed beyond the realm of human emotions and reactions and is equated with "shimmering, intermittent light" (*parisphuranta*) which is being revealed in a sudden "flash" (*pratibhā*). And in this commentary Abhinavagupta specifies that Sarasvatī here is yet another name for the goddess of Speech (*vāk*), while a "sudden flash of light is consciousness which shines forth anew in each its scintillation."[50]

One recalls that in *Tantra-āloka* ("The Light of Tantra") Abhinavagupta was already writing:

> Indeed, when he [hears] sweet songs,
> or when he touches sandal-wood,
> When he is no longer [content]
> with staying in the middle,
> [and being indifferent],
> when a tense vibration (*spandamānatā*)
> [starts] in his heart,
> Then it is called the power of bliss

---

48. See *Locana*, 1.6, where they are characterized as bringing forth *ānanda-rasa* or the ontologically coloured "passion of bliss."

49. Ānandavardhana, *Dhvanyāloka*, 1.6: "arthavastum alokasāmānyam abhivyanakti parisphurantaṃ pratibhāviśeṣam /"

50. Abhinavagupta, *Locana*, 1.6: "pratibhā apūrvavastu nirmāṇakṣamā prajñā /"

and this man becomes
the "same-hearted" one (*sahṛdaya*).[51]

The same "power of bliss" (*ānanda-śakti*) which in poetry corresponds to *rasa*, is placed here in a broader context: aesthetic pleasure, or aesthetic passion, is regarded as an ontological category, as a basic feature of the universe (and not only a quality of a literary work). Or, to approach it from a different angle, it is the world itself that becomes a poetical text created or expressed by Speech. Then, of course, it becomes clear that, according to Abhinavagupta, the order of significance is reversed. It is not the clever "connoisseur" who is capable of understanding *rasa*, but, rather, as soon as the passion of *rasa* becomes "recognized," he, who succeeds in this "recognition," immediately becomes equal to the poet, becomes the "same-hearted" one (*sahṛdaya*).

This brings us to the last problem relevant to Abhinavagupta's aesthetics. Can one really say that in his system the message that reaches the addressee is essentially one and the same, regardless of the letters, their authors, and recipients? Or, in other words, is it possible to maintain that Abhinavagupta's *rasa*, or "ontological passion," is basically one and the same, regardless of the texts through which it is conveyed?

Of course, everything depends on the interpretation of that *rasa*. As we could see, it is by no means to be regarded merely as an instinctive emotional reaction to a cleverly chosen stimulus. Rather, it is emotion itself that becomes a haphazard locus, a "place" for the manifestation of *rasa*, an indication or mark of its presence. In the words of Abhinavagupta's *Locana* (1.5),

---

51. Abhinavagupta, *Tantrāloka*:

Tathā hi madhure gīte spṛśe vā candanādike /
Madhyasthyavigame yāsau hṛdaye spandamānatā /
Ānandaśaktiḥ sauvoktā yataḥ sahṛdayajanaḥ /

Tantra-āloka, ed.
with notes by Rajanaka Jayaratha,
vol. 2 (Bombay, 1920), 200.

> grief (*śoka*) is a "persistent mood" (*sthāyi-bhāva*) which becomes an essential sphere for tasting the [*rasa* of] "compassion" (*karuṇa*). And since the state of consciousness (*citta-vṛtti*), which [is defined by] the impulses (*vibhāva*) and effects (*anubhāva*) as regards to the persistent mood of grief, becomes the appropriate *rasa* when it [reaches] the essence of tasting, it is possible to say that the [man who] stays within [this persistent mood] attains the *rasa*.[52]

As it was said in *Dhvanyāloka* about the very "first poem" of the very "first poet," Vālmīki (who was supposed to have uttered the first verse lines depicting the grief of the male krauñca-bird after the death of his female companion), the poem itself conveys not the grief but something entirely diffrent. The message which is sent out by the poet and received by the listener deals with an entity quite unlike the usual emotion we might experience in similar circumstances of real life. Grief itself is being superceded by something else; to be the real factor of a transformation which is about to take place for the listener, it should itself be radically transformed. It is no longer a psychological state, no longer a "state of mind"—changeable and malleable—but something that might be terned a true κάθαρσις, that is, a sudden glimpse, a sudden "flash" (*pratibhā*) of a new ontological reality.

And now, coming back to the problem of the message: since the main purpose of the work of art seems to be its ability to open a window through which both the poet and the listener can have a glimpse of a new entity (which, incidentally, coincides with their own true nature), would it not be right to assume that the message always essentially remains one and the same—regardless of the concrete poetic examples that serve it as a pretext? Of course, if one sides with Bharata, who

---

52. Abhinavagupta, *Locana*, 1.5: "karuṇasya tac carvanāgocarātmanaḥ sthāyibhāvaḥ / śoke hi sthāyibhāve ye vibhāvānubhāvās tat samucitā cittavṛttis carvyamāṇātmā rasa ity ocityāt sthāyino rasatāpattir ity ucyate /"

enumerated eight major *rasas* and practically equated them with corresponding emotions, that can hardly be the case. But if one faithfully tries to follow the inner development of Abhinavagupta's thought, then, I think, one is bound to agree that the aesthetician was definitely looking for one principal *rasa*.

At the first glance, his break from Bharata seems hardly significant. It is well known that Abhinavagupta added a ninth *rasa* to Bharata's list; it became known as the *rasa* of "peace," "tranquility" (*śānta-rasa*) (Ānandavardhana introduces this *rasa* in the third chapter of his *Dhvanyāloka* [3.26], but he does not offer any detailed explanations for doing so). With Abhinavagupta, the introduction of the ninth *rasa* is something that immediately changes the whole perspective, something that shifts the whole angle of approach used for the analysis of the other eight *rasas*. As it is said in *Locana* (3.26) about the *śānta-rasa*, "since it is founded on the higher goal of men (*parama-puruṣārtha*) because it [brings forth] the fruit of liberation, it is considered to be the basis (*pradhāna*) of all [other] *rasas*."[53] One must say, however, that there is an exceptionally perceptive passage dealing with *śānta-rasa* in the fourth chapter of Ānandavardhana's *Dhvanyāloka* (4.5):

> The goal of men, defined as liberation, is [regarded] as the only higher [goal] in the *śāstras*, while in poetry it is the *rasa* of peace (*śānta-rasa*), defined as the blossoming of happiness brought about by the quenching of thirst. . . . Since it is the main essence, its meaning can only be conveyed by suggestion (*vyaṅgyatvena*) and not by literal means (*vācyatvena*). And indeed, the meaning of the main essence shines forth much more beautifully when it is not conveyed literally, in [ordinary] words (*svaśabdānabhidheyatvena*). And it is agreed, whenever the skilful and the wise are convened, that a highly regarded object shines

53. Abhinavagupta, *Locana*, 3.26: "mokṣaphalatvena cāyaṃ paramapuruṣārthaniṣṭhatvāt sarvarasasebhyaḥ pradhānatamaḥ /"

forth when it is being conveyed by suggestion and not directly (*na sākṣāc*), not through [ordinary] words.[54]

Probably the most important passage concerning *śānta-rasa* is to be found in Abhinavagupta's commentary on Bharata's *Naṭya-śāstra*. There it is directly likened to the higher *ātman*, and the attainment of this *rasa* is clearly understood in terms of the cathartic transformation of ordinary reality. In the words of Abhinavagupta, when one wants to know the nature of aesthetic pleasure,

> it is said thus: *ātman's* own nature is being [temporarily] colored by "laughter," "erotic love," etc. that can tint it into their own hues. But, [all the same,] he remains this extremely white [colorless] thread which shines (*nirbhāsamāna*) through the conglomeration of loosely strung [semi-transparent coloured] jewels. It assumes the shapes of all emotions like erotic love, etc. [that are superimposed upon it], since all these emotions can tint it into their own hues. But it still flashes forth (*vibhāta*) through them as soon as the knowledge shines (*bhāsamāna*): "this is *ātman*." It is devoid of the conglomeration of sorrows which consists of turning away from it. And since it is the attainment of the higher bliss (*parama-ānanda*), it shines forth (*nirbhāsamāna*) whenever there is an "idealization" (*sādhāraṇatā*) [of emotions] in poetry and drama. And owing to this distinguishing of the direct perception it [transforms] the heart [of the listener] into an abode of this over-worldly bliss."[55]

---

54. Ānandavardhana, *Dhvanyaloka*, 4.5: "mokṣalakṣaṇa evaikah paraḥ puruṣārthaḥ śāstranaye kāvyanaye ca tṛṣṇākṣayasukhaparipoṣalakṣaṇaḥ śānte raso / . . . atyantasārabhūtatvāc cāyam artho vyaṅgyatvenaiva darśito na tu vācyatvena / sārabhūto hy arthaḥ svaśabdānabhidheyatvena prakāśitaḥ sutarām eva śobhām āvahati / prasiddhiś ceyam asty eva vidagdhavidvatpariṣatsu yad abhimatataraṃ vastu vyaṅgayatvena prakāśyate na sākṣāc chabdavācyatvena /"

55. Abhinavagupta, *Abhinavabhāratī*, 6: "ucyate uparāgadāya-

In other words, it is *ātman* itself that, using the "suggestive" language means as its medium, transforms both the poet and the listener into "same-hearted" (*sahṛdaya*) addressees for the message of Speech.

And, finally, another curious point which seems to be quite significant for Abhinavagupta. Even insisting so uncompromisingly upon the predominance of the *śānta-rasa*, he still inserts in his commentary on the *Dhvanyāloka* a short verse which presents the *rasa* of peace in a slightly different light. The verse was written by Abhinavagupta himself, and it goes as follows:

> Oh you, the moon-crested
> Lord of the living breath,
> when you touch me suddenly
> after the long pain of separation,
> My consciousness—
> a doll carved of moon-stone—
> melts and melts away.[56]
> (*Locana*, 3.30)

Here, as Abhinavagupta himself is ready to acknowledge, all the skilfull devices used in order to produce *śṛṅgāra-rasa* or the *rasa* of erotic love, are implemented for the sake of awakening *śānta-rasa*. It is just another reminder that one should not take

---

bhiḥ utsāharatyādibhir uparaktaṃ yad ātmasvarūpaṃ tad eva viralombhitaratnāntarālanirbhāsamānasitatarasūtravad yad āhita tat svarūpaṃ sakaleṣu ratyādiṣu uparañjakeṣu tathābhāvenāpi sakṛdvibhāto 'yam ātmeti nyāyena bhāsamānaṃ parāṇmukhatātmakasakaladuḥkhajālahīnaṃ paramānandalābhasaṃvidekatvena kāvyaprayogaprabandhābhyāṃ sādhāraṇatayā nirbhāsamānaṃ antarmukhāvasthābhedena lokottarānandānayanaṃ tathāvidhahṛdayaṃ vidhatta iti /"—*Abhinavabhārati*, vol. 1, p. 339.

56. Abhinavagupta, *Locana*, 3.30:

Tvāṃ candracūḍaṃ sahasā spṛśantī prāṇeśvaraṃ
gāḍhaviyogataptā /
Sā candrakāntākṛtiputrikeva saṃvidvilīyāpi vilīyate me //

the "*rasa* of peace" at its face value; in other words, one should not fall into the trap of "literal" meanings (*abhidhā*). The most "peaceful" of all Abhinavagupta's *rasas* has an unmistakable flavor and sting of erotic passion.[57] Just like any other *rasa*, it is first and foremost an ontological "passion," that is, a real and dangerously alive energy (*śakti*, ἐνέργεια), a pulsating tension (or, if one wishes, "melting away") which is endlessly at work, endlessly pushing forward, ever bent on looking for consenting partners in order to renew and reiterate its eternal dialogue.

---

57. D. H. H. Ingalls very aptly (if paradoxically) describes this "*rasa* of peace" in his introduction to the translation of the *Dhvanyāloka* when he says: "The one thing that *śāntarasa* does that no other *rasa* can, is that it disturbs us." See *The "Dhvanyāloka" of Ānandavardhana*, p. ix.

The Name and the Voice: Some Concluding Unscientific Remarks

So, as we have seen, according to the writers of early Vedānta tradition, the higher reality is presented in the form of some language (or sonoric) entity which is basically fourfold. Both Gauḍapāda and Bhartṛhari do their best to enumerate several of the "foursomes" that constitute various manifestations of the higher Speech: the main sets of elements that are named by them include, among others, the "stages" (*avasthā*) or the "steps" (*pāda*) of consciousness, the cosmic aspects of the higher Brahman, the forms or levels of speech itself, the phonetic elements of the sacred mantra *Oṃ*, and so on. . . . In any event, whatever the explanation or substantiation offered, there decidedly seem to be too many of these sets. In fact, in order to avoid fruitless speculations, in order not to be drowned in the endless discussions concerning the respective degree of "reality" of all these foursomes, and, finally, in order to escape the enumeration of countless correspondences between the "microcosm" and the "macrocosm," I suggested taking an entirely different approach.

Instead of dealing with an indefinite number of actually existing sets of "elements," we are confronted here with a kind of energy field which is giving birth over and over again to one and the same pattern, to one and the same configuration. Then the elements themselves can no longer be regarded either as real or unreal, and the only ontological reality present is that of an energy wave itself, of an inner tension that is persistently bent on producing the same structure. The whole of the universe is evoked due to the pulsation, "shimmering" (*span-*

ditā, sphoṭa, sphurattā, kampa) of this pattern which is ever oscillating between manifestation and latent contraction. In early Vedānta of Gauḍapāda and Bhartṛhari, Brahman itself is being equated with this imminent vibration of the higher Speech, which is ever ready to burst forth into a fourfold dynamic structure.

There was also a tentative explanation offered for the shape and general outline of this energy pattern which seems to be invariably splitting into four elements with one of them clearly set aside and occupying a somewhat privileged position. It was suggested that the first three points represent the inherent division of speech itself, when, remaining the absolute subject, the absolute "I" of the dialogue, it addresses the interlocuter, the absolute "thou," while speaking and naming something that is ever destined to remain the "third person," or the object of the conversation. Then the fourth element is bound to represent the silent, primordial stage of Speech (*vāk*) which lies beyond the boundaries of that dialogue, embracing it and simultaneously supporting it from within.

It was further maintained that the concept of language energy as the foundation of the universe, the image of Speech as the only possible ontological base for any existing entity, as well as the only possible gnoseological instrument for any valid knowledge, was by no means an entirely unique feature of early Vedānta systems. Its direct continuation can be traced in the ideas of non-dualist schools of Kashmir Śaivism, while some striking parallels came to be singled out within the fold of Neoplatonist and Hesychast ideas. To my mind, the most close similarities with Gauḍapāda's notion of "vibration" (*spanditā*) and Bhartṛhari's concept of the sudden "flashing out" (*pratibhā*) or "recollection" (*pratyabhijñāna*) of the higher reality are to be found in Abhinavagupta's version of Śaivism (the Pratyabhijñā school, or the school of "recognition"), as well as in his aesthetical ideas concerning the interrelation of *dhvani* and *rasa*.

Meanwhile, the reader may have noticed that I mostly tried to avoid discussing the erotic connotations of the theory of Speech energy (*vāk-śakti*)—connotations which were, in fact, quite relevant for Śaiva Tāntrism. Of course, there is an extensive literature—both in Sanskrit[1] and in Western languages—dealing with this by no means unimportant subject. But this omission itself is, perhaps, in its own way rather significant. Strictly speaking, the same mechanism was already set to work as soon as we tried to approach the innermost point of absolute being or absolute consciousness: the shadow of this ineffable entity was immediately thrown upon the nearby ground, creating a sort of limbus, a peculiar space shunning concrete definitions. One might remember in this respect that both in Vedic texts and in the Sanskrit treatises on poetics it was always emphasized that the most important core, the most deeply engrained entity should remain carefully evaded and unnamed. Something precious enough to be sheltered might be hinted at, touched upon, but never forcibly penetrated: "Since the gods somehow like indirect and hate direct [naming]."[2]

The development of the early Vedānta ideas within the fold of Kashmir Śaivism clearly shows that the very element of language was always regarded as a highly erotic medium (something that any artist trading in words would probably agree with). The medium supporting the relationship between the artist and the spectator, the poet (*kavi*) and the "same-hearted" listener (*sahṛdaya*), is initially charged with erotic tension; by its very nature it is basically the same element and the same medium that brings together the lover and the beloved. The agents engaged in the relationship are themselves unimportant, it is the vibrating charge of love and mutual

1. The subject got itself quite exhaustive treatment within the framework of the Kaula school of Kashmir Śaivism, in particular, in the works of Jayaratha (especially in his commentary on *Tantrāloka* ("The Light of Tantra"), 5.121-24, 29.104-6, etc., though, of course, this angle was always important for the followers of the Krama and Trika schools, including Abhinavagupta himself.

2. The already cited passage from the *Bṛhadāraṇyaka Upanishad*:

Parokṣapriyā iva hi devāḥ pratyakṣadviṣaḥ /
(*Bṛhadāraṇyakopaniṣad*, 4.2.2)

recognition, equally ripping them open for one another, that really counts. For Gauḍapāda and Bhartṛhari, the separate elements in the structure of the world are irrelevant and interchangeable, it is the pulsating interplay between them that bears all the significance. And for the Śaivite Tāntrika adept Abhinavagupta, the synchronized reverberation of *prakāśa* ("pure light of consciousness") and *vimarśa* ("dynamic self-reflection") is already tentatively presented as erotic union.

At the same time it should be borne in mind (and it is certainly true for non-dualist Kashmir Śaivism) that the most universal paradigm for erotic love is already preset in advance by the relationship which binds together God and the living soul. Incidentally, from the point of view of religious experience, every and any kind of love is essentially and inescapably "love that dares not speak its name," and precisely because of that every kind of love is meant to be jealously and superstitiously safeguarded by elusiveness and shame.[3]

Viewed from a religious perspective, love which is shorn of its secretiveness and shame is fated to remain at most a healthy exercise that might keep one fit or contribute towards procreation but is scarcely capable of approaching ontological reality in the same right as religious passion. In exactly the same way, language which is shorn of its connotations, suggestive and ambiguous meanings will always remain a handy and useful scholarly tool that is scarcely capable of creating new images and new worlds.

And Abhinavagupta would have said that what is being "recognized" is never an object of love itself (since both God

---

3. In this respect it is equally important, for example, that Christ's death on the cross—which for us will always remain the highest possible expression of love—represented an execution which was meant to be not merely a painful and tormenting one but an essentially shameful one as well. Religious love seems to bear the imprint of this ultimate shame and secret. One might remember that, according to S. Kierkegaard, the highest religious stage was that of the *troens ridder* ("the knight of faith"), who would never consent to be named or acknowledged as such, who was ever supposed to remain "incognito."

and the animated, cognizing subject are essentially placed beyond the grasp of knowledge) but the overwhelming ontological passion, or *rasa*. One is immediately aware of the presence of *rasa* (or *pratibhā*—the "flash" of light) owing to that specific "trembling," "shivering" (*vīp*)[4] that overtakes both the poet and his listener, bringing forth the overtones of erotic love (*ullāsa*) and joyous amazement of recognition (*camatkāra*). The amorous union of Śiva and Śakti, the intermittent red-and-white glow inside the primaeval "dot" (*bindu*), is not just a reminiscence of their fecundity—after all, we cannot really know whether the universe born of this love is ontologically real or not, whether, in fact, the creation had ever taken place.

---

4. The Vedic verb (*Ṛg-Veda*, 10.99.6) implies the ecstatic trembling that inevitably accompanies poetical inspiration. In fact, it was something quite akin to the "divine madness" (θεία μανία) of Plato; and, according to him, this "madness" is essentially of four types: one afflicts "prophets" or "philosophers" (they are protected by Apollo); one, "religious initiates" (they are looked after by Dionysius); one is the destiny of "poets," who depend on the Muses; and the last is reserved for the "lovers," who stay within the domain of Eros and Aphrodite (See *Phaedrus*, 265b, 2-5. One can also recall, that in his "*Second Manifest of Surrealism*" (1929) André Breton reminds the reader of the similar "passionate madness" (*furor*), referring to the same four kinds of it, only taken in accordance with a Neoplatonist version (André Breton, *Second manifeste du surréalisme.*—André Breton, *Oeuvres complètes*. Vol. 1. Paris: Gallimard, 1988, p. 820). The coincidence here is by no means accidental: it is well known that Breton was genuinely fascinated by mediumistic trances and other trans-psychic, "twilight" states of consciousness. The surrealists' interest in psychodelic transformations of consciousness was mainly due to their attempts to gain entrance to the so-called "automatic writing," that is, to the moment when some inner foundation of artistic creativity starts to "speak forth" instead of the person himself. Of course, from the surrealists' point of view, this foundation is identical with "subconscious mind," with deeply buried layers of consciousness, which remain obscure for us and underlie the structures of the conscious self. And Bhartṛhari and Abhinavagupta would have said that even this "automatic writing" is ultimately dictated by higher Speech.

The pulsating vibration of this union is first and foremost to be regarded as essentially elusive, secretive tremor of erotic and artistic passion.[5] The medium of language, the element of Speech, is highly erotic because only language proves to be truly capable of both concealing the meanings and simultaneously suggesting them by way of that very concealment.

In terms of Hesychast theology, we cannot be ultimately transparent either for ourselves or, for that matter, for God Himself, since otherwise the concept of eternity would lose its meaning, being replaced by the picture of endless and repetitive boredom. And according to Abhinavagupta's aesthetics, when something is being repeated (and the poet never really generates new language, he can only bring forth something that is already inherently present in the language structure), it is invariably done as if for the first time, as if anew, in wonder and amazement. The elusive point (*bindu*) of artistic creativity is always wondrously unpredictable, yet it is reached through language, it makes use of language means, and is developed inside its very nature. The artist's task is not to "copy" or "imitate" the universe but to make full use of his creative energy (theologically speaking, he should not be concerned about the "anology of being" but only about the "analogy of act"). Actually, in Abhinavagupta's aesthetics, the main function of an artist is primarily a theurgical one, and artistic creativity is yet another simile (or "reflection," *pratibimba*, or even "play-

---

5. One of the most prominent theoreticians of French surrealism, Marcel Duchamp, used similar images when analysing the nature of art. According to him, our soul is mostly open to the potential creative impulse not in the moment, when we try to invent something totally new. Creativity reaches its height when the artist willingly agrees to become a medium for an energy wave, for a field of force that insists on "speaking" through us. It seems that artistic gift is ultimately measured by the willingness to surrender to the beckoning call of this power. Incidentally, Duchamp's concept mostly reminds us of one of the favourite Śaivite images: in the moment of the union with the Godhead there is a reversal of sexes, and a male adept has to meet the higher entity with submissive trembling of femininity.

ing out," *naṭya*) of the creative impulse rooted in the very origin of the universe. The initial moment of shivering tension, the moment of creative urge is bound to remain inconceivable, it is never meant to be understood or named, though one can certainly try to find the appropriate names for the relations, links, and lines of force that come to be manifested when the higher Brahman, which is simultaneously the higher Speech, suddenly starts to swell and split up from within.

Poetical means devised by language itself bring us closer to the eternally evasive core of existence and consciousness, because they are endowed with power (*śakti*) to convey the meaning without directly naming it.[6] And when we suddenly "recognize" something that is present only as a hint, as an indirect reference, we experience an unexpected outburst of aesthetical rapture which brings us closer to the ineffable "essence" (οὐσία). With every creative effort of the poet we come closer to the resonance of energies, that is, closer to the solution of the ultimate puzzle.[7]

While trying to focus the attention on "consciousness" or "speech" as the foundation of the universe (including all the

---

6. When Martin Heidegger was saying: "Worte, wie Blumen," he did not actually mean that words were "like" flowers, that is, he was not referring to their "beauty," "exquisiteness," or something like that. What was implied here was the fact that they do essentially function, do behave "in the same way as" flowers, that is, that they are equally capable of blossoming, bursting forth with new shapes, forms, and meanings. See Martin Heidegger, *Unterwegs zur Sprache*, 206.

7. In his book on the concept of *dhvani*, S. J. Anand Amaladass translates the basic term as "symbol." While I do not really agree with this interpretation, one of his observations seems to be entirely pertinent. He reminds the reader that the Greek verb συμ-βάλλειν originally meant the trick of bringing together two parts of a broken ring, stick, or plaque in order to identify the messenger (see S. J. Anand Amaladass, *Philosophical Implications of Dhvani. Experience of Symbol Language in Indian Aesthetics* [Vienna, 1984], 140). In fact, *pratibhā* or the "flash" of enlightenment, *pratyabhijñā* or "recognition," and *rasa* or ontological, cathartical passion, happen when

means and devices of poetical language), one can sympathize with Jacques Derrida's emphasis on "writing" (*l'écriture*). In his system it comes to be presented as a silently implied foundation of all human culture and philosophy. In quite an interesting work, "Derrida and Indian Philosophy," two chapters of which deal with correspondences between Derrida and Bhartṛhari, Harold Coward tried to show that any mutual ground for these two thinkers should be sought primarily in the concept of the dynamic nature of language.[8]

Of course, it is important to determine—or, at least, to approach—the inner foundation of one's cultural assumptions, the inner base of thought and reasoning. However, from the point of view of early Vedānta philosophers, what we ultimately get after accomplishing all the "deconstructions" is not "writing,"—even taken in its most archetypal form—but rather the living and dynamic "Speech that speaks" ("*vāc . . . vakti*"). Or, to bring it even closer to the original etymologies, what we get is the "Voice" (*vox*, *la voix*) which is endlessly and tirelessly persevering in its invocations and vociferations, trying to capture our attention with its own devices—the "Voice" which is capable of convoking or evoking images, the "Voice" that is ever intent on continuing its activity within us.

---

all the randomly scattered pieces suddenly come to fit together, thus enabling us to solve the puzzle.

8. See Harold Coward, *Derrida and Indian Philosophy* (Albany: SUNY Press, 1990). Coward finds the parallels between Derrida and early Vedānta in Derrida's idea of mental "trace," "imprint" (*la trace*), which precedes every development as something that introduces *la differance* or the power to distinguish, to separate (to make "different" in space and "to defer" in time). For him it seems to be quite consistent with the notion of the "driving force," the inner "potency" (*śakti*), in particular, with the notion of the "power of time" (*kāla*) that urges, pushes (*kalayati*) things forward, forcibly makes them happen (H. Coward, *Derrida*, 40-42).

Index